A Poetics for Screenwriters

A Poetics for Screenwriters

Lance Lee

University of Texas Press, Austin

First edition, 2001

Requests for permission to reproduce material from this work should
be sent to Permissions, University of Texas Press, Box 7819, Austin,
TX 78713-7819.

ⓧ The paper used in this book meets the minimum requirements of
ANSI/NISO Z39.48-1992 (R1997) (Permanence of Paper).

Library of Congress Cataloging-in-Publication Data

Lee, Lance, 1942–
    A poetics for screenwriters / Lance Lee.—1st ed.
        p.   cm.
    Includes bibliographical references.
    ISBN 0-292-74718-7 (cloth : alk. paper)—ISBN 0-292-74719-5
    (pbk. : alk. paper)
        1. Motion picture authorship.   I. Title.

PN1996.L39   2000
808.2'3—dc21   00-036415

[P]laying, whose end, both at the first and now, was and is to hold, as 'twere, the mirror up to nature, to show virtue her own feature, scorn her own image, and the very age and body of the time his form and pressure.   Hamlet, *Hamlet*, III, 2

[S]ometimes the little world succeeds for a moment in reflecting the big world, so that we understand it better. Or is it perhaps that we give the people who come here the chance of . . . forgetting for a while the harsh world outside.

Dear, splendid actors and actresses, we *need* you all the same. It is you who give us our supernatural shudders and still more our mundane amusements.   Oscar, then Gustav Adolf, *Fanny and Alexander*

Contents

Introduction ix

I. Context
1. The Fundamental Story Pattern 1
2. The Creative Root 7
3. Drama's Continuity 13
4. Film and Dramaturgy 20
5. Audience Relations 25

II. Primary Plot Elements
1. Screenplay Defined 30
2. Where Stories Come From 32
3. The Nature of Conflict 34
4. Location, Scene, Sequence 36
5. Starting Stories: Establishing Character and Conflict 39
6. Starting Stories: Choosing Material and Treatment 40
7. Backstory, Preparation, and Exposition 42
8. Complication, Major Reverse, Minor Reverse 44
9. Discovery and Its Types 47
10. The Dramatic Obstacle, Change and Suspense 49

11. The Beginning: Development of the Dramatic Problem   50
12. The Middle: Development to the Crisis   54
13. The End: Climax and Resolution   57
14. Revelation, Clarity, Truth   60

III. Dramatic Reality
1. Emotions Make Real   62
2. Identification, Empathy, Sympathy and Fascination   63
3. Story, Dramatic, and Running Times   65
4. Cause and Effect: Immediacy and Meaning   66
5. Necessary and Probable   68
6. Irrational Improbable Elements   70

IV. Storytelling Stance and Plot Types
1. The Action: Point of Attack   75
2. Plot Complexity, Types, Variation, and Magnitude   76
3. Dramatic Unity: Relating Subplots and Parallel Plots   79
4. Typical Story Patterns   81
5. Narration, Flashback, Fragmented Action   85
6. Exceptions   86

V. Character
1. Sources and Types   88
2. Force, Consistency, Change, Truth   91
3. Defining Character   92
4. Building and Revealing   95

VI. Mind in Drama
1. Ideas and Innovation   99
2. Theme in Action   101
3. What Structure Is For   102
4. Creating Values and Moral Urgency   104

VII. Spectacle and Other Elements
1. Spectacle and Special Effects   107
2. Music and Sound Effects   109
3. Dialogue   111

4. Symbol and Metaphor   114
5. Dramatic Irony   116
6. Comedic Turns   117
7. Adaptation   121

VIII. Developing and Filming the Story
1. How Stories Really Develop   124
2. Premise, Treatment, Stepsheet, Storyboard   126
3. Production Facts of Life   128
4. Last Things: Manuals, Formats, and Perseverance   130

Notes   133

Screenplay Author List   137

Introduction

A Poetics for Screenwriters remedies the lack of a concise summary of all essential aspects of the screenwriter's art and its place in society, the psyche, and the history of drama. No such text exists at present despite the many manuals, textbooks, specialist writings, individual memoirs, and collections of essays on the market. Some manuals, although short, omit significant aspects of the art in order to present a particular method. *A Poetics for Screenwriters* presents not another method but an overview of the essential elements that both a beginner and a professional should find useful within whatever method they may prefer. Only Aristotle's *Poetics,* written 2,400 years ago and focused on Greek tragedy, offers such an overview of the dramatic art. Unfortunately, Aristotle's work needs constant updating as another class or professional is baffled by remarks on Greek vowels while intrigued by those on the types of discovery or the nature of a Reverse.

Screenwriting is our dominant dramatic form, the heart of film, the quintessential twentieth- and now twenty-first-century art. It is time screenwriters had their own, modern Poetics. My approach is to show and summarize all important dramatic elements of screenplays clearly and succinctly without bias, not to prove and guide, though an understanding and mastery of these elements would mark anyone as a fine writer. Examples are drawn from many national screenwriting traditions, including works by Bergman, Kurosawa, Kieslowski, Wallace and Kelly *(Witness)*, Williams *(A Streetcar Named Desire)*, Schulberg *(On the Waterfront)*, and many others. Drama cuts across boundaries and binds diverse screenwriters and cultures.

Students and teachers will find *A Poetics for Screenwriters* useful as a supplement in beginning classes and as a fundamental text on which to expand in advanced. Professionals will find a pointed review of an endlessly fascinating and rich art.

The sections that follow are often cross-referenced, as in "I, 2," to give easy access to related or supportive material. A sentence or quote followed by a superscript numeral refers the reader to the Notes section, which has been kept to a minimum to maintain a professional focus and brevity, and appended to the text. My claim is to bring together, not to originate: all I claim for myself here beyond the wit of brevity is that "modesty is all."

A list of the films mentioned, and their screenwriters, is also appended. A number of classic plays are used, since a screenwriter is the heir to 2,400 years of dramatic undertakings; these are appended and listed also.

Finally, scenes referred to from *Kramer vs. Kramer, On the Waterfront, A Streetcar Named Desire, The Graduate, The Godfather,* and *Fanny and Alexander* are quoted in full in *The Understructure of Writing for Film and Television,* the textbook that I and my colleague Ben Brady take responsibility for, also from the University of Texas Press.

A Poetics for Screenwriters

I Context

1. The Fundamental Story Pattern

Modern man arrives on the evolutionary stage with a creative explosion. Our stone tools show a new variety, complexity, and beauty, while the great cave paintings like those at Lascaux and Altamira, or the even earlier works from parts of the world other than Europe, are our first memorable achievements. Some paintings in other parts of the world are eighty thousand years old. The creative response to experience is so deep-seated in us that we often equate creativity with health and its absence with illness. When anyone, at any age, looks at anything or does anything in a healthy way, he or she is being creative.[1]

Drama, like all the great arts, rises from a fundamental engagement with our experience. Whatever size an individual's particular gift may be, that gift is only a matter of degree of our common creative response to reality. We may praise Shakespeare or Sophocles or a contemporary screenwriter like Bergman as being "one of a kind," but that is just the hyperbole earned by great work.

Great screenwriters belong in the same company as great dramatists: screenwriting is only our own current variant of playwrighting. The 2,400-year-old dramatic tradition is as much a screenwriter's heritage as a playwright's. For the last fifty years much of the greatest dramatic writing has been for the screen.

Consider our great cave paintings. If we enter one of the famous caves illumined by modern standards, we see fixed but startling representations of wildlife that cover the walls, sometimes with images painted over one another, sometimes mixed with the images of hands, or of "wizards." We don't know whether these paintings simply aim to give pleasure through illusion or involve sympathetic magic to gain power over a chosen animal in the hunt, whether the animals represent a celebration of the natural power and fecundity of the world or are part of some kind of religious rite. We are impressed but feel we are in the presence of a lost world.

But imagine that we use our ancestors' weak, flickering lighting instead.[2] Now the animals *move* on the walls in an interplay of light and shadow; some lead us deeper into the cave. Some caves have a broad outer chamber, then a second that narrows until a person can barely squeeze forward, imagining the great weight of stone about to crush him, until he drops suddenly into a third and final small chamber with a sense of relief and revelation. There he is confronted with stones and bones that suggest an altar and a lost rite.

No one knows what kinds of rites were practiced in these caves, if any. But imagine a rite in such a trying setting, perhaps one of initiation: a boy entered the cave, underwent the mysterious rite, and emerged a man. Or a girl entered, and left a woman. Neither was ever the same again. A purposeful movement in response to a felt need, moving through a broad beginning to a tightening and ultimately frightening middle, then reaching a final climactic release, after which all is changed, is the fundamental pattern that we still find in our dramas.

We still undergo that journey in a dimly lit cave.

It is still a social, public event.

Consider the pattern. An individual, who exists at a certain point in time, has a problem—in our hypothesis the onset of puberty (the past). He or she *must* undergo an experience, a ritual, to mark the change psychically and socially into adulthood (present action). He enters the large cave, perhaps accompanied by others, is oriented, and then encouraged to go on alone. His choice to do so propels him into the narrowing tunnel; the constriction excites a sense of claustrophobia, the endless stone a sense of danger; his courage is threatened, a sense of crisis builds, yet he doesn't dare stop, but squeezes forward. Abruptly he drops into a small, open chamber. Men in animal furs and masks await him; an animal is sacrificed, or celebrated. Whatever is done, is done, and when he emerges, his life is now a man's life, or if a woman, a woman's. The experience changes either forever (a new beginning).

Past: Present Action: New Beginning. The problem(s) existing in the past are resolved in the course of resolving the immediate difficulties of the rite, *or the story,* and a new start is made possible.

Consider *Star Wars.* Darth Vader's corruption by the Emperor, the Emperor's corruption of the Empire, Obi-Wan's role as inadequate teacher, and the rebellion in which Princess Leia plays a key role exist before the action begins. Luke knows little of these circumstances, certainly not that he is destined to help set things straight. These problems from the past emerge and intertwine with the present problems that Luke faces, complicating the issue and raising the stakes, until by the end of the film he saves Leia, defeats Vader, destroys the Death Star, becomes a hero, and starts on the path to become a Jedi Knight.

Julie in *Blue* doesn't know her husband has been having an affair before he and her daughter are killed in an accident at the story's start. She has lived a lie, ignored Olivier's love for her, and encouraged the world to think her husband a great composer. She is considerably more than a muse, but has denied helping her husband actually compose. The immediate action forces her to find a new life for herself, and as she does so the problematic past emerges and intertwines with her immediate goals. By the end of the film Julie accepts Olivier's *true* love, discovers her husband's pregnant mistress, and gives her forthcoming child the inheritance of Julie's late husband. Now, it is implied, Julie will compose for herself. Past and present culminate in a new beginning.

In the past of *On the Waterfront* Terry became a bum after taking a dive in a major fight that he could have won, betrayed by Johnny Friendly and his own brother, Charley. Unrelated events years later lead Terry to discover a conscience and to turn on the corrupt Johnny Friendly and demand from his brother, in one of the most famous scenes in screenwriting, the right to make up his own mind. He reproaches Charley for having let him down before: "I could have been somebody," he says. "I could have been a contender." Not a bum. By film's end he becomes somebody by heroically taking the union from Johnny Friendly.

Charlie, in *Roxanne*, has long believed he can't be loved for himself because of his disfiguring nose. That conviction emerges into the immediate action as he falls in love with Roxanne, yet helps Chris win her after Roxanne falls for Chris and asks his, Charlie's aid to win Chris! Roxanne is deceived in Chris, thinking she has finally met someone with poetry and intelligence, just the sort of man she is looking for at the beginning of the film. Comedically, it is Charlie who has those qualities. By film's end the truth is revealed, and Roxanne loves Charlie for himself, nose and all.

Robert Towne's *Chinatown* holds in the past a complex tale of incest, betrayal, land-grabbing, and greed, all problems that Jake Gittes stumbles onto as the story unfolds. All are resolved by an end that finds Gittes a changed, enlightened, and saddened man.

Decades of crime and hope, including the intention for Michael to have a noncriminal career, predate the start of *The Godfather*. But other Mafia families are jealous of the Corleones, and a conspiracy against them is set in motion in the immediate action when Don Corleone refuses to help Sollozzo introduce the drug trade into the Mafia. By the end of the film, drugs are in, the conspirators assassinated, the "family" base of operations moved from New York to Las Vegas, and Michael the don.

Glory is based on the Civil War experience of the Massachusetts Fifty-fourth Infantry, a black regiment. Southern and racial intolerance generally, and the Civil War, already exist in the past when Colonel Shaw is asked to train the first black regiment. In the immediate action he discovers that racial prejudice exists within the Union Army itself. He repeatedly overcomes obstacles to have his men treated fairly and used legitimately on the battlefield, but at the cost of his own and many of his soldiers' lives in the climactic assault on Fort Wagner. Yet by film's end the Fifty-fourth has proved its ability and heroism and, for itself, overcome racism.

Marshal Kane in *High Noon* is a newlywed leaving town when the film starts, but a sense of duty forces him to turn back to confront vengeful men returning from his past, from prison, to kill him. One by one, those who should help Kane betray him, until at the Crisis he stands alone on Main Street as his former mistress and his wife ride past him to the railroad station.[3] He triumphs in the showdown with the help of his bride, who returns at the last moment. In a famous scene at the end he tosses his badge in the dust at the feet of the cowardly townspeople and leaves. The past has been overcome in the immediate action, which revealed the true nature of the townspeople, and a new life has begun.

This fundamental story pattern has an additional feature. While the past and the new beginning stretch before and after the action, we see *that the immediate action itself falls into a clear beginning, middle, and end sequence.*

Philadelphia detective John Book detains the recently widowed Amish woman Rachel and her son, Samuel, in *Witness* because Samuel has witnessed a murder. Book discovers that past corruption and drug money are involved as he searches for the killer, including his own captain. Book is wounded: his, Rachel's, and Samuel's lives are in danger. He flees with them to their home among the Pennsylvania Amish, where they cannot be easily traced. End of the Beginning.

Rachel nurses Book back to health, and they fall in love. He becomes involved in Amish life, yet he is always aware that its pacific values are at odds with those of the "real world" that he represents. When he learns that his partner has been murdered in Philadelphia, he gives himself away in an act of violence that allows the corrupt police to find them. End of the Middle: Crisis.

Climactically, Book triumphs in an extended action sequence over those intent on killing him, Rachel, and Samuel. He has the choice of taking Rachel with him to Philadelphia, or staying with her among the Amish, but he leaves alone, realizing that their values and lifestyles cannot mix. End, and resolution.

We could go through any film and find the same structure in the immediate action. That structure accords, in a suggestive, formal way, with the sequence of the imagined rite in the cave. If it is not an instinctive way of organizing experience into stories to render meaning, then it is so deeply embedded in our culture that it might just as well be.

Like all patterns or "rules" in drama, variations exist, as in *A River Runs Through It,* where the past outside the immediate action is reduced to insignificance by virtue of its dramatization in the first part of the film: the Beginning contains both this dramatized "past" material and the actual beginning segment of the crucial, decisive summer on which the film focuses. These exceptions are rare, and serve to confirm the prevalence of the pattern, extending and modifying our understanding, while never contradicting the Beginning, Middle, End structure of the immediate action.

Thus defined, the fundamental story pattern in drama is the existence of more or less unknown problems before the beginning of the immediate action that are drawn into that action step by step and ultimately resolved with the immediate problems. The audience is usually ignorant of these key past elements except in the case of well-known stories or myths; usually the hero and heroine suffer from similar ignorance. As our hero and heroine, or protagonists, struggle to resolve immediate problems, they discover the existence of pre-existing problems whose resolution is necessary in order to resolve their own immediate problems. The hero and heroine also discover that those earlier problems are fundamental to a true understanding of their lives, and to the creation of a new beginning. Their struggle, the immediate action of the film, falls into a clear beginning, middle, and end. The Beginning contains the immediate problem(s) that generate the story, into which past elements intrude. At the end of the Beginning, the protagonists believe they now understand those problems and can see (or stumble into) a line of action to deal with them. The Middle is that line of action followed until it seems to or actually does collapse, thus constituting the Crisis. The End is the final, tightly focused action taken in response to the Crisis, in which our hero and heroine climactically succeed, and resolve all difficulties, or fail, and resolve all difficulties. The unknown is now known, the problematic resolved, the protagonists transformed, a new beginning found.

The action of the drama is an engine of transformation.

Along the way we are entertained by the characters' struggles, enlightened by their fates, and given a vicarious sense of wholeness by their resolution of the conflicts in their lives. We experience their new beginning vicariously as our own.

The engine is for us.

It hardly matters whether we weep along the way or laugh our heads off.

2. The Creative Root

Professional screenwriters grow uneasy when the terms "creativity," "art," and "artist" are bandied about: their eyes glaze over when yet another aesthetic or psychoanalytic interpretation begins. Screenwriters are professional, practical, and commercial. If pushed, they will admit to being dramatists; to go further smacks of pretension and impracticality. Hollywood is certainly as mercenary a place as can be imagined.

But drama accords to real needs beyond the current conditions of writing and making or staging films and plays: it has fundamental roots in psyche and society. A screenwriter who is unaware of the issues involved is blind to the depth and richness of his art.

Aristotle postulated instincts of imitation, and of harmony and rhythm, to explain the mimetic nature of all art.[4] Imitating is pleasurable in itself, as is the expression of harmony and rhythm, and while Aristotle is at pains to focus on tragedy, it is clear that we can be pleased by a simple entertainment involving a well-done imitation of an action, with appropriate elements of harmony and rhythm. Many of our films are no more than entertainments of this kind; some are only platforms for musical sound tracks.

There is a dark side to harmony and rhythm, and though Aristotle avoided it, our modern experience makes that avoidance impossible. Rhythm and harmony can be hypnotic, and can take individuals out of themselves. Imagine the occasional riotous rock concert; imagine Nazi torchlit spectacles with their mass marches and rhythmic chants. Rhythm is an avenue to the irrational, which we often equate with amorality, destructiveness, madness, and death. Much as creativity may spring from an irrational or unconscious or nonrational root, so too may destructiveness.

Aristotle reduces the irrational to story improbabilities, and lists ways to rationalize these (III, 6), yet admits that metaphor is inexplicable, a matter of "genius."[5] Although he tries to understand metaphor as a literary device, all dramatic writing is a metaphor and springs from "genius"—that is, from other than simply conscious roots. Whenever we write a story, we make a claim for its reality, its representation of people in difficulties that must be worked out, though all of that is imaginary and is presented through a complicated technology. The claim of one thing to be another is the claim of metaphor.

Plato gives a telling metaphor of the fundamental forces from which our art grows in the Phaedrus, with its famous analogy of the soul to a charioteer harnessed to black and white horses.[6] The black horse is pure desire, constantly threatening to overturn the chariot, altogether lacking in self-control. The white horse responds to the charioteer's commands readily, eager but measured, self-controlled. It is a pregnant metaphor for the mind that still resonates with its vision of conflict or, as we might put it, with its vision of the ego struggling to balance passionate instinct and conscience.

A good deal of what we see in films accords with this struggle to bring the excesses of passion into a new, harmonious balance. In The Godfather it is greed that upsets the peace, and an attending lust for power. Michael slowly discovers that his task is to bring the consequences of these unbridled feelings into control in a new synthesis. He wins that synthesis, but at the price of his own corruption. If we start to look at stories from this angle, we find that this struggle to contain passionate error in a new synthesis is one of the deepest sources of drama's grip on our imagination: the dramatic story functions as an unconscious ritual of conciliation.

Nietzsche takes this further with his famous definition of Apollonian and Dionysian impulses.[7] Apollonian art is the art of the dream—imagistic, ordered, harmonious, structured, individualistic, ultimately self-aware. Dionysian art is the art of ecstasy, excess, passion, self-forgetfulness, of the swept-away lyrical poet (or rock star), unstructured, anti-individualistic and asocial, the movement of the spirit that bridges our evolutionary split with nature by unifying the unconscious and conscious minds. If we amplify this beyond aesthetic definitions to evocations of two tendencies in the mind, we uncover a forceful way of thinking. Revealed on the one hand is a tendency to erect a structured, meaningful, bounded, coherent life, individually and as societies; on the other is an urge beyond ourselves, sweeping, emotional, nonrational, a force that brushes aside Apollonian constructs, at once destructive yet also clearing the ground for a fresh beginning after old structures have ossified.

We will always be caught between these urges, always be seeking some degree of measure with passion so that we do not feel alienated from our own roots, always, in short, find ourselves seeking to balance order and disorder, reality and illusion, structure and freedom. We will always be charioteers harnessing our own opposed drives and needs.

Consider *High Noon*, where only Marshal Kane is not subject to uncontrolled passion, whether of fear, revenge, disappointed self-esteem, or envy. He certainly feels fear, but is not mastered by it; he feels anger, but does not surrender to it. He holds himself together, upholding an individual and social principle of duty, an Apollonian hero par excellence who triumphs over the destructive forces symbolized by the returning gunmen. His final gesture of contempt leaves behind the spineless, deceitful, envious townspeople that he thought were his friends.

Emotional Apollonian and Dionysian transactions like these are endemic in drama, another root of its staying power in our culture and in the urge of individuals to invent the metaphor of a film's action that allows audience and writer to experience such symbolic, psychic conciliations.

In this sense we can understand viewing each tragic hero in classical Greek tragedy or each hero in contemporary drama as essentially one hero, the man who confronts the upsurge of the passionate, inexplicable, and sweepingly irrational thread in self and society or nature that threatens to sweep away the individual. The hero is our stand-in, the person who stakes out an area where the individual can survive in some comprehensible haven, however illusory or compromised that haven may be, as in films like *Witness* or *The Godfather* or even *Independence Day*.

Carl Jung's notion of the psychic archetype of the hero gives a modern psychological version of this idea, where the hero's tale is a metaphor for ego integration.[8] He must slay monsters as part of his labor, representing the unbridled unconscious, in order to win a state of balance and integration where life is possible. Such heroes stand mythologically at the doorway to civilization in many cultures, men who rise to the occasion, find and slay the monster, liberate or find the heroine, and through their marriage with the heroine symbolize the wholeness of the mind (Jung) or the establishment of a civil order (myth), which less troubled generations can then enjoy, until that order ossifies and needs itself to be swept away or renewed, at which time a Dionysian force stirs again.

So we can put a fresh spin on Kane in *High Noon* or Detective Book in *Witness* or Michael in *The Godfather,* or on Luke (and Han) and those supporting the "Force" in general in *Star Wars.* They deal with corrupt environments where "monsters" are on the loose. Their success is a cleansing and a taming that makes civil society possible, or at least the society of the "family" in *The Godfather.* Lest this seem far from the working reality of professionals, remember the close relationship between Joseph Campbell and George Lucas, or the far more basic fact that these forces and acts of conciliation exist daily, moment by moment in our own minds. Screenwriters are particularly gifted at expressing such conflicts through their stories.

A utilitarian side of drama is contained in Aristotle's purgation theory. The purpose of tragedy is to purge the emotions of fear and pity. So purged, he implied, the members of the audience felt tragic wonder and made better citizens because they were able to make unclouded judgments. Nietzsche thought that the tragic solace and elation resulted from the sweeping away of the Apollonian hero by Dionysian forces that led us, through our identification with the chorus, to the perception that life is indivisible and eternal (I, 5). We know that drama cuts a wider and deeper swath than these thinkers credited, because it is not only tragedy that reaches such meaningful effects. At the same time we know that these effects in our films are transitory, require repetition, and rarely have immediately beneficial social results, although they always satisfy existing emotional needs within our psyches and culture.

We have taken inherent, creative structuring forces in ourselves for granted since the great dispute between David Hume and Immanuel Kant that created modern thought.[9] Hume showed that our normal concepts of time, space, and cause and effect could not be deduced from experience. The only things that experience could show were duration for time, mere area for space, or sequence in place of cause and effect. Kant thought we could hardly live without our concepts of time, space, and cause and effect, and he rescued these from Hume's skepticism by showing that they were innate structuring tendencies in the mind without which coherent experience would be impossible. Research has long since showed that our senses sift and select among sensory data, so what we see and hear and taste and smell and touch are constructs; Kant reminds us that our minds are equally active sifters and constructors of cognitive experience. From his point of view, to experience at all is an innately creative act.

That ability must wrestle with the irrational, destructive urges in us that our own century has laid bare so starkly. Our modern psychologies swim around these perceptions in their own ways, some seeing creativity as innate, some seeing it as growing out of experience as a reaction to destructiveness. Creativity baffled Freud, who tended to see it as a sublimation of more fundamental drives, like the libido (sex). In later thinking he saw the libido as opposed to the destructive urge, which in the thought of Melanie Klein, one of his most influential descendants, became the death wish. She saw creativity as flowing from a desire to repair imagined damages from early fantasy. Jung saw creativity as a separate complex on a par with any other.[10]

Yet all depth psychologies miss the point to the extent that they don't see creativity as fundamental, for all without exception speak of the power of fantasy and assume it to be operative from the earliest age. As we grow, our fantasies are disciplined, tested, discounted, or confirmed by reality. What begins as fantasy we later call play, and we play from infancy. D. W. Winnicott perceived that "on the basis of playing is built the whole of man's experiential existence."[11] And he pointed out that play quintessentially leads into the cultural area, that critical part of all our experience which is not wholly me nor wholly you, but is the place where you and I meet and interact, the area that stories inhabit, where films are made, and audiences sit together to share imagined experiences. Screenwriters are only disciplined play-artists.

Consider again the fundamental story pattern that typifies our films. The lingering problem from the past is a clue that an existing reality is not what it seems, that a presumed balance struck between Apollonian and Dionysian, creative and destructive, ordering and dis-ordering forces is an illusion. The hero and heroine discover as that past problem enters the immediate action that they have been living a lie and must put something new and more true in its place. They survive multiple mistakes as they struggle to do so until the final Crisis and Climax test and reveal their uttermost capabilities: they triumph (usually), and a new beginning or life opens based on a firmer grasp of reality, on a sustainable tension between passion and control.

Drama, once discovered in history, with its immediacy, its characters in conflict who stand in for ourselves, its problem-solving orientation, is an ideal form for these needs to be given body and allowed, harmlessly and vicariously, to play out.

This is the fuel on which the "engine of transformation" runs.

Some of our creative response to reality we accept on faith in received religious or secular structures, while these remain effective, but a significant amount we accept from our artists, who deserve that title because it takes real artistry to satisfy such continuous psychic needs and to fashion a critically respected, effective, commercial piece of storytelling. Every screenwriter sets out to do so. Every screenwriter has the profound, if unconscious interest of an audience in his ability to do so. Every screenwriter is an artist of urge and restraint, instinct and license; of conflict and conciliation; Apollonian and Dionysian; a charioteer harnessing difficult steeds, rite-inventor, monster-slayer, civilizer, integrator, and entertainer at once. Otherwise drama would shrink in significance, lose its vast funding and distribution, and rarely be attended, instead of being our constant fare on television and in the cinema. The studios would vanish, cinemas would be rebuilt for other uses, and their equipment consigned to junkyards. We would never think of a great dramatist as one of our great men.

3. Drama's Continuity

The film medium for drama is new, but the effects that screenwriters are better able to realize in film are old, as are their dramatic instincts and the essential structure of effective drama. Even our contemporary screenwriting style is heir to a revolution in dramatic taste and practice in the late nineteenth century. The dramatic heritage that is a screenwriter's by right offers a huge practical resource of examples by previous dramatists wrestling with the stuff of human conflict from farce to tragedy, yearning for and sometimes achieving cinematic effects. Yet too often contemporary screenwriters are ignorant of their birthright, to their own impoverishment.[12]

Devices like asides may seem typical of Shakespeare, but *Alfie* is largely a series of asides. Cinematic spectacle seems uniquely contemporary, yet what surpasses the Watchman in Aeschylus's *Agamemnon*, performed in an outdoor amphitheatre, greeting the dawning sun as the beacon signaling the end of the Trojan War? The camera may draw us in on spiders crawling on Indiana Jones in *Raiders of the Lost Ark*, but does that have any more impact than Aeschylus's chorus of Furies costumed with such snake-crowned verisimilitude at the start of *The*

Eumenides that they sent the Athenian elite in the front row into panicked flight?

Greek tragedy pioneered the essential dramatic realities that we still use under its surface format of alternating segments of choral performance and action, which explains the continued relevance of Aristotle's *Poetics*. Tragedy rose from a chorus of satyrs, men costumed as creatures who were men above the waist but goats below, who celebrated the reincarnated god, Dionysus. Don't think of satyrs as absurd figures: the Greeks saw them as symbols of natural, true man, one still in unity with nature. Soon the satyr chorus split into audience and performers: then Thespis (hence our "thespian") introduced an actor (one who literally carries out an action) to interact with the chorus. Aeschylus and Sophocles added additional actors, which led to drama through the development of dialogue and scenes of action between actors.

The resulting tragic plays were staged in a contest (*agon,* hence our "agony") at the Great Dionysia, the spring religious festival, and the best was given a prize. Aeschylus portrayed men like gods, Sophocles idealized men, and Euripides showed men as they are. The Climax of tragedy did not result in gloom but in the ecstatic solace and perception of the communal continuity of life sparked by the fate of the masked tragic hero, at once individual and generic (I, 2). But that solace faded, and tragedy died under the impact of Socrates and other philosophers who emphasized reason and debunked the traditional myths used by tragedy. No entire tragic plays survive after Euripides.

The later new comedy of Menander, the subsequent Roman comedy of Plautus and Terrence, and the literary tragedies of Seneca owed most to the passionate yet rationalistic drama of Euripides. But these died too in the later Roman Empire as mime and the gladiatorial and animal contests of the arena supplanted them.

Drama, when it loses its ability to connect with our fundamental psychic needs, can become superficial to the point of irrelevance and then vanish. There is no guarantee of renewal even when renewal is needed.

Our own drama was born similarly through religion, specifically from the Latin liturgy of the Church in the Middle Ages. By the tenth century the "Quem Queritus Trope" existed, wherein three women stepped forward at the appropriate moment in the service to question the angel at Christ's sepulcher about His rising from death. Dramatic episodes soon burgeoned in number and turned more mundane until they were driven out of the Church onto cathedral porticos. Plays were now performed against the spectacular backdrop of the great cathedrals, while their stage juxtaposed multiple sites: the terrestrial paradise, hell, and, in the cathedral, heaven. The result was a spectacular performance, as fluid as that of a film.

Drama soon moved into the marketplaces, courtyards, and secular courts. Great cycles of plays developed, some taking days to perform, a few still currently performed in Europe. Traveling troupes, keyed to the religious calendar, performed largely secular plays on great two-story wagons containing on a lower level prop and dressing rooms, and on the upper, stages. Audiences moved past one stage to another, or watched them roll by, each with a different part of the action; narrators on horseback made the connections. Actors mixed with the audience, hawkers sold their wares, children and animals rushed among the crowd, while some watched from their windows or, if nobles, from horseback, in a noisy and spectacular scene. Extravagantly expensive productions did not originate in Hollywood: medieval guilds were sometimes threatened with bankruptcy as they vied to mount ever more spectacular productions. The public taste for such entertainment is as old as theater, innate to drama, always threatening the balance between truth and spectacle that drama has to maintain.

Morality plays performed in much the same way supplanted the mystery cycles after the religious Reformation in England and Europe: it is likely that Shakespeare saw some of these as a child. He was heir to a complicated compromise developed in England between the native epic and popular traditions of morality plays, the popular secular farces that had split off from these, and the Renaissance attempt on the part of university men to revive classical tragedy. In Europe the Renaissance attempt to re-create Greek tragedy by fusing action and music led to the creation of opera. But for Shakespeare and his contemporaries, the Roman Seneca with his fevered oratory and bloody action was considered the great classic model. The resulting Elizabethan fusion of sources, a crucial root of our drama, led to an often tragicomic style that mingled elevated and common, sublime and farcical, tragic and ridiculous elements in a style close to the confusions common to reality.

Thus Hamlet mocks the players as they ham up speeches in *Hamlet,* or pauses at the graveside to remember Yorick, playing with his skull, while Polonius is at once absurd and touching. Jeff, in *Rear Window,* has Miss Torso and the newlyweds to amuse him as he tries to catch a murderer. Bottom and his compatriots ham it up in comedies like *A Midsummer Night's Dream,* while the aristocrats stumble around in a confused, more elevated daze. Charlie alternates dealing with farcical firemen and the brilliant Roxanne in *Roxanne.* Henry V has as his bosom companion the comedic Falstaff, while Luke is accompanied by a set of Laurel and Hardy robots in *Star Wars.* Plays like *Measure for Measure* and *Much Ado About Nothing* give a standard tragicomic shape to drama: after a dramatic testing the good are rewarded and the bad punished, our favorite choice as well as that of the Greeks and the Elizabethans.

We routinely adapt Shakespeare to film because both his stage—an apron thrusting out into the audience with a minimum of scenic resources—and his audiences demanded a continuous flow of action.[13] Like a contemporary screenplay, Shakespeare's plays were written and performed without scene or act breaks: these were added by later, literary publishers. The texts were pruned to allow a two-hour performance, while the imagination made up for the lack of scenic resource: "imagine we are on the field of Agincourt, in the castle of Elsinore, near Athens." Recent film versions include Kenneth Branagh's *Henry V, Much Ado About Nothing,* and *Hamlet.* New versions of *Twelfth Night, Othello,* and *Romeo and Juliet* have appeared. A screenwriter with as many immediate credits would think himself on a roll.

Even cinematic effects were anticipated by a vogue for immense painted dioramas in the eighteenth century, spun on great drums across proscenium stages to the delight of ecstatic audiences a century before anyone began to think of film technology. That technology developed swiftly from the serial photos of Muybridge in the 1860s and the single-camera sequences of Marey in the 1880s to Edison's Kinetoscope, which, by 1893, was using rolls of coated celluloid film. The Lumiere brothers developed their Cinematographe by 1895, and a year later projection machines like the Pantopticon and Vitascope were in use in the United States. The first shop to show only movies opened in Los Angeles in 1902, and by 1905 the first movie theater was in operation. It charged a nickel, and hence was called the Nickelodeon. Ten years later the age of the silent film was in full swing, and men like D. W. Griffiths were creating the first film masterpieces.

Cinema offered a new medium for the appearance of drama that greatly increased the importance of producers and directors, changed the nature of acting, and complicated the role of screenwriters (VII, 1; VIII, 3). Productions were as swift as those on the medieval or Elizabethan stages, substituted the camera for the imagination, and reduced the role of the first screenwriters by the absence of sound. Once "talkies" began, the screenwriter's role grew, though the static nature of early sound equipment led to "stagy" dialogue, and the previous emphasis on production led to a system where writers were regarded as dispensable, easily replaced or supplanted. But a new style developed with the development of sound technology that was at once spare, swift, and focused on telling, closely observed actions. As film has grown up, the importance of a writer's undiluted vision of the action has steadily increased.

Yet our current screenwriting dramaturgy doesn't derive primarily from film but from the new dramaturgy developed by the Norwegian playwright Henrik Ibsen, who bent the theatrical revolution inspired by naturalism in the late nineteenth century to his own ends. The theater of Ibsen's day had atrophied: between Sheridan and Shaw in England there is a century-long gap of forgettable drama, while in Europe, despite such late explosions of romanticism as Rostand's *Cyrano de Bergerac*, the stage was predominantly under the sway of slight, well-made farces and comedies by playwrights like Scribe and Sardou. Naturalism, inspired by the Industrial Revolution and propounded by

Emile Zola, then adapted by Ibsen, transformed the scene. The film medium absorbed Ibsen's revolution in dramaturgy and honed it after the advent of the "talkie" because its popular, realistic appeal is congenial to the illusion of reality that the camera creates, and it accords with our middle-class democratic tastes.

Naturalism calls for a scientifically truthful drama: real flesh-and-blood men and women should be in real stories drawn from immediate reality. Individuals should be shown as determined by heredity and environment, and morality brought into the modern world: how is anyone to be blamed for what he cannot control? The dramatist should be the objective portrayer of this situation, avoiding well-made plots, contrivances, and romantic or inflated incidents that obscure the truth. He should use epic and narrative features, including "slice of life" stories, because drama should echo the flowing, casual stream of life. This is Aristotle's "drama is an imitation of an action" notion given a contemporary, plotless spin. Even superfluous events or characters are justified in the name of verisimilitude. Finally, the audience should be assumed, or ignored, not consciously played to. Nothing is better suited than film itself for such an approach: by the time an audience sees a film, only images of the actors remain.

Ibsen absorbed and changed this as he wrote the first realistic feminist, environmental, and psychologically deterministic plays, the first showing the negative role of ideology, the first equating fate with medical heredity. Then he wrote the first quasi-symbolic plays as he moved past realism into the kind of dramaturgy suggestive of another great Scandinavian, Ingmar Bergman. Ibsen died in 1905, the same year the first nickelodeon opened.

No one had ever encountered a drama of such immediacy as *A Doll's House,* in which, for the first time, a married couple discuss their marriage in normal conversational idiom, and the wife, Nora, rejects all her husband's conventional but deeply felt moral and religious arguments in order to go off and find herself and the truth.[14] Ibsen rejected the governing mores of his time and implied that a society that held half of humanity (women) in bondage did not deserve respect or continued existence. The result was a critical storm whose virulence we can hardly imagine (VI, 1). If a screenwriter wrote a film with such an impact today, he would be profoundly pleased, if not amazed. That a film like *Kramer vs. Kramer* was greeted simply as a good movie indicates the tremendous gulf of practice and outlook that we have crossed in a short time.

Ibsen's stories are well plotted. Slices of life held little appeal for him. The individual is someone he wanted to vindicate, not show at the mercy of blind forces, as in naturalism. He sought a poetry of dramatic action: the acts of *A Doll's House* are written as unbroken streams of action. Typically, there is a significant past event that determines present action, as in Nora's counterfeiting her father's signature in order to get a loan to save her husband's life, which took place before the immediate action of the play. If fate exists (as in naturalism), it isn't exclusive: it is in addition to other dramatic elements.

Ibsen uses traditional devices like letters, plot turns based on props, the use of knocks on a door to herald entrances and action leading to reversals. If he were writing today, split-screen telephone conversations or messages on answering machines overheard by key characters would be elements in his stories, while a contemporary score would replace significant knocks.

Characters should have representative, defining acts, like Nora's surreptitiously eating forbidden macaroons. Dialogue must reveal character, advance the action, display irony, and be presented in normal conversational idiom. Productions should show a detailed verisimilitude. In *On the Waterfront* Ibsen would have liked Terry's playing with his longshoreman's hook as he listens to Edie berate him for thinking of going back down to the docks, or his putting on the jacket of Edie's murdered brother, which by now symbolizes repentance and revolt (VII, 4). The extreme realism brought by the camera to the setting would have pleased him equally.

Subplots, often parallel, were as acceptable to Ibsen as to John Michael Hayes in *Rear Window,* or to Shakespeare. Nora loses her husband in *A Doll's House,* while Christina gains one. Lighting should be used symbolically, as Tennessee Williams uses it in *A Streetcar Named Desire* in the famous movie version with Marlon Brando. At a key moment Mitch tears a cover off a light to reveal Blanche's true face and age. The ideas in a story—and stories should have ideas—should be unified with the action: theme, in other words, should emerge through what is done (VI).

Imagine, for a moment, that we removed Ibsen's practices from current screenwriting: very little would be left.

4. Film and Dramaturgy

Raiders of the Lost Ark starts with views of the Peruvian jungle: as the titles follow, we draw in on Indiana Jones making his way along a jungle trail.

Tsar Ivan tries to succor his sick wife, Anastasia, in Eisenstein's *Ivan the Terrible:*

> Ivan rushes to Anastasia,
> to give her a drink,
> to bring her relief.
> He turns to the beaker beside her.
> The beaker is empty.
>
> He stumbles, he twists—he seeks everywhere for water.
>
> Carefully Euphrosyne stands her cup in the path of Ivan.
>
> She looks out of the corner of her eye at Malyuta:
> Malyuta notices nothing, he is plunged deep in thought.
>
> Ivan snatches up the cup.
> He carries it to the Tsarina.
>
> Euphrosyne conceals herself in a corner. She watches from the corner.
>
> Anastasia drinks thirstily from the cup.
> Her eyes are wide open in fear.
> Ivan holds the cup solicitously . . . [15]

In the corner Euphrosyne secretes away a vial of poison.
The opening montage of Jean Cocteau's *The Blood of a Poet* begins:

> The author, masked except for his eyes, holding a plaster hand
> in his hand, this real hand and the wrist of the other covered
> by draped cloth, announces that the film is beginning, against
> a backdrop of studio lamps.
>
> Between the credits, the text, the dedication and the prologue,
> there is a close-up of the knob of the door that someone is
> trying to open.
>
> A huge factory chimney. It leans over. It begins to crumble.
>
> The author's voice: *"While the cannons of Fontenoy thundered in
> the distance, a young man in a modest room . . . "*
>
> We hear the cannon. We see a young man drawing at an easel.[16]

Note the beginning of *Raiders of the Lost Ark.* Entire travelogues
are built around exploring particular natural areas. Here we see a real
jungle, albeit one actually filmed in Hawaii, not Peru, as the titles
claim: shortly thereafter we see not *National Geographic* explorers but
Indiana Jones searching for an archaeological treasure. The illusion of
reality is powerful: real people appear to be in a real jungle; why
shouldn't everything else be real?

*Film lets us confuse reality and imagination more easily than any
other dramatic medium.*

Look at the scene from Eisenstein. We move around the characters,
Ivan giving his wife a drink (a close angle), Euphrosyne giving Ivan a
cup (a wider angle), Euphrosyne glancing at the pensive Malyuta (two
close angles), or Ivan taking the cup to Anastasia (another angle). We
spy on the most intimate details, see the most casual nuances, and
sense the meaning through the varying sizes and durations of the
images.

*Film makes us intimate viewers, even voyeurs. The camera is our eye,
and knows no barriers.*

Note two further characteristics: representative, defining action, and a whole given by nuance, and their emotional power. "The beaker is empty. He stumbles, he twists—he seeks everywhere for water." What is conveyed is Ivan's emotional urgency, not just the absence of water. Then Euphrosyne "looks out of the corner of her eye at Malyuta." We see that sidelong glance and know immediately that she is plotting, which is a much larger reality than simply glancing at someone. Terry gives two classic instances of representative action as he listens to Edie in *On the Waterfront* (I, 3).

The placement of the camera and the details it chooses communicate significance and feeling.

This is true even for great emotional weight: we don't need a grand confrontation like the trial scene of Thomas More in *A Man for All Seasons* to create such weight, though the fusion of such scenes with spectacle adds a further heightening. Screenwriters have learned since the fusion of sound and image in the 1930s to eliminate dialogue and monologue where the sense and emotion of an action can be revealed more immediately and powerfully by just such physical, symbolic acts as Euphrosyne's glance or Ivan's stumbling.

Look at the opening of *The Blood of a Poet.* The modern camera combines apparently real images for any setting or action with the fluidity of dream. Those images can be realistic, like the start of *Raiders of the Lost Ark,* surreal, like Cocteau's opening, or fantastic, like those beginning Lucas and Kasdan's *Star Wars.* Nothing about such images prevents our belief in a story's reality. It is only a step from the surreal to the dreamlike, and dream sequences are not unusual in films. Yet all we ever see on the screen are filmed sequences of imaginary action, whatever their style, equally dependent on the mind's credulity before what the eye sees. We are very credulous, indeed: we will accept the reality of anything we see so long as it has consistency and a story to which we can relate (III, 1).

Film lets us shape reality more completely than any other dramatic medium.

Writers have always written rhythmically when writing well, whether they are writing sequences cutting back and forth ever more quickly between scenes of action as they move toward a climax, drawing out a moment to increase tension and anticipation, or finding a moment of calm after an outburst of frenetic hilarity. Such rhythm is a kind of "music" that exists above and beyond an actual score, one that is present in all films, whether conventional or those by directors like Bergman or other, usually European, filmmakers who eschew the typical Hollywood sound track (VII, 2).

But the camera powerfully augments the expression of dramatic rhythm with its fluid shifts of location and emphasis on chosen details, as when *The Godfather* intercuts a baptism with multiple assassinations, at one moment emphasizing baptismal water, at the next, splattering blood.

Film makes dramatic rhythm viscerally visible.

Finally, consider the climax in *Witness* as Book confronts the corrupt police. Much of a film's rhythm is created by the director and the editor as they determine which shot to use and how much of it is needed to convey the necessary action. But the writer first conceives that action, the stages of its development, and its essential rhythm or pacing. Book struggles to get the car going. He hears footsteps and drops into a lower part of the barn. The animals grow restless, Book flees. He discovers a dead end in the corn silo, retreats, then climbs in and up. He is still for a long, painful moment in its upper darkness as a killer stares upward but cannot see him. Then Book loosens a plank and drowns the killer in corn. Desperately he digs out the gun and shoots McFee, who has rushed toward the sound of the drowning man, only to be confronted by Captain Schaefer holding a gun on Rachel. Hysteria grips them both: Book lowers his gun to save Rachel. They step outside and are confronted by a crowd of Amish. The captain can't kill everyone; he turns away and sags to the ground, defeated.

This is like listening to the final movement of a sonata: a crescendo, a momentary lull; a renewal of a drive toward climax, another relative lull; then . . . During this sequence the movement of the camera, or our eye, lets us move in close with Book, certain that he will be shot, and then see the top of the silo, where Book is lost in darkness, from his hunter's angle, blending swift action with intimate detail and nuance, maximizing emotional impact.

Seeing and writing work hand in hand for the screenwriter: the action is as much something seen as heard; a screenwriter writes behavior more than any other dramatist.

The screenwriter's tools to create illusion overwhelm our imagination and give a scope to the adage "actions speak louder than words" that was barely glimpsed by Ibsen. The screenplay format allows screenwriters to make use of these tools as they visualize the action. But, as a practical note, a finished script should not have the six hundred or so shots that a production script will have. That much detail makes it unreadable; the script should include only those shots that locate the screenwriter's visualizations and underscore the key moments.

We see these stories in our modern "caves," dimly lit auditoriums with capacities that vary from less than a hundred to thousands. Often they are clustered together in a house of illusions where crowds gather, bent on the same social experience in neighboring locations. Facing us in these auditoriums are screens that vary in size but are always big enough to show larger-than-life images. Before a film begins, the lights dim, ads appear, we are "entertained" by a demonstration of the sound system that has been installed for our greater pleasure, and previews (future illusions) run. Finally the feature starts. We view a jungle in "Peru." . . . We are in the Tsar's palace. . . . Naked women dance about with guns, and the James Bond theme begins. . . . Joanna's face from *Kramer vs. Kramer* fills the screen. . . . Alexander drifts about in a house, as a statue shifts position in *Fanny and Alexander*. . . . We are soon caught up in some variation of the fundamental story pattern. . . .

Actually, something quite different happens.

Images of actors projected on a blank screen perform actions that have already been completed in the production of the film: everything we see is aftermath. It has no immediacy at all. Nor is anyone moving. Instead still photos flash by at a rate of twenty-four a second, tricking our eyes into "seeing" motion. The sound is on a separate track added much later to the visualizations. Special effects, many of which no actor ever saw, have been interpolated into the action: the characters move among computer-generated images of rooms, spaceships, dinosaurs.

At a stage performance live actors perform immediate actions before our eyes. In contrast, film is like a dream image, an Apollonian construction of illusion, a conscious dream already dreamed and now repeated for our entertainment. Studio stages and the computer-generated visuals deepen the gap between reality and image.

Worse, like children, we confuse size with significance: big images of even common people doing ordinary things must mean that both have a larger-than-life importance. What a Greek tragic actor needed elevated boots, a mask, and myth to achieve, we do instead with a technology that exalts the commonplace into the generally significant. Joanna, in *Kramer vs. Kramer,* her face filling the great screen, stands for all unhappy women in all unhappy marriages driven to desperation.

A screenwriter needs to remember that in terms of reality there is little to choose from between Cocteau's *The Blood of a Poet,* Eisenstein's *Ivan the Terrible,* Lucas and Kasdan's *Raiders of the Lost Ark,* and Benton's *Kramer vs. Kramer:* they are all equally deceptive illusions of the first order, differing only in their outward styles. Yet we are so easily deceived, that film surface is so compelling, and our urge to believe runs so deep, that we will believe in a reality we know is all smoke and mirrors unless the story is too flawed to hold our assent.

That is an incredibly important power at a screenwriter's disposal.

5. Audience Relations

These reflections lead to some unexpected realizations. The "Fourth Wall" theory invented by Jean Jullien as naturalism swept the stage at the end of the nineteenth century created a new relationship between the audience and a play. Actors were to imagine that the proscenium arch held a wall ensuring their privacy, while those in the audience were to imagine that they looked through a window into lives that were unaware of their presence. How else could scientific objectivity be gained, stagy artifice avoided, or a "slice of life" accurately presented? Unobserved, crippled, Jeff spends much of his time peering through his window into lives that go on in other apartments in John Michael Hayes's *Rear Window:* in the Fourth Wall concept, we are all voyeurs like Jeff.

Film is the ultimate Fourth Wall and also its cancellation. The action appears on the literal wall of the screen, making the illusory claim to "reality" and "immediacy," although technically it is neither; simultaneously, the camera's fluidity appears to draw us into the settings and lives of the characters with a privileged anonymity and unparalleled intimacy. We are there.

We are there passively.

Earlier dramatic forms invited our imagination to provide the setting. Film spares us the trouble. By and large we accept what we see, and believe more firmly in that reality than in the one suggested by an actual stage. The machinery of film illusion is overwhelming (I, 4). We are unseen viewers of a ritual, playgoers whose imagination is fed, not challenged to supply realities that a stage machinery is too primitive to emulate: France is before us, or Peru, or the Tsar's palace, or the bedroom shared by Joanna and Ted. We are acted upon, and we need do nothing but watch.

Three important considerations follow for the screenwriter from these facts:

First, as we saw above, all styles are styles of illusion: real, surreal, symbolic, or fantasy; the prevalence of any style is a result not of its being more or less inherently real but of the audience's taste; what varies least is the fundamental story pattern, which can be told in any style to equal belief.

What is this pliable belief that is so easily guided?

Children, and those unfamiliar with drama, believe a play or film to be absolutely real, like the Maoris in *The Piano* who seek to intervene because they believe someone onstage is really in danger. We believe what we see and hear, as our birthright, instinctively; that will to believe is always with us. Realizing that a dramatic story is just a story is a learned and sophisticated response, that Nietzschean qualification to the Apollonian artist who creates a beautiful, moving action, yet knows in the back of his mind it is an illusion that is as real, but no more so, as a dream.

Screenwriters are disciplined dreamers.

Second, our will to believe functions unimpaired as a story begins, or we could not believe at all. But, adult and corrupted with knowledge, we know that all that seems real is not, and so we are saved at the last moment from the terror of complete belief in the vengeful tyrannosaur in *Jurassic Park: The Lost World.* Yet some part of us believes it is real, and for a time we let ourselves go, hungry for the lost innocence of unquestioned belief, the ground from which all stories rise, from which myth gains its power to embody a believable crystallization and explanation of experience. That is why we believe movies can do so, too. Only later do we think, Ah, yes, it was just a story.

In short, a mythopoetic drive is instinctive in us, and visible everywhere.

Third, Einstein may have developed a theory of relativity: we, shortly, developed the social theory of relativity, the notion that "everything goes." Newton may have set modern physics on its way, but very soon deism developed his ideas into a mechanical worldview. Darwin's ideas were elaborated into social Darwinism, a conservative social philosophy, still with us, that buttresses unbridled capitalism. We constantly elaborate the "facts" into these explanatory systems; we cannot help ourselves. Drama does so as well, knowing it is creating an illusion that will draw strength from our hunger to believe.

This powerful will to believe feeds in at the beginning of every story. Where are we, we ask; who is there, and why; why do they stay there, what problem keeps them there, what do they do about it? A screenwriter who answers these questions for the audience coherently and consistently can take anyone on any journey he pleases. This will to believe has deep implications for beginning a story, too: we need time to be oriented through the answers to those initial questions, however dramatically we start, before we go anywhere with any set of characters (II, 5–6). A simple film under Lucas's aegis, *Radioland Mur-*

ders, illustrates this point, for it never takes the time to draw us in, or to give us a moment to catch our breath during its run; as a result, the story never jells, and the film fails.

Suspending disbelief is another matter. Disbelief only becomes an issue when a writer stumbles and belief begins to falter.

Finally, we need to ask ourselves, Where does the action of the story happen?

One of the virtues of Nietzsche's theory in *The Birth of Tragedy* is the way in which he focuses on the relation of the audience to the story. At first, in the development of tragedy, the audience and the celebratory chorus of satyrs were the same. Then the chorus split off; the audience watched and listened, no longer being direct participants, and identified with the chorus. As actors split off from the chorus and the dramatic action was born, the audience still identified with the chorus, which was physically and psychically interposed between the audience and the actors. The chorus stood in for the audience. How, then, did the action appear to the audience? As the embodied imagination or dream of the chorus, which the audience saw through the chorus, given physical presence by the actors. Hence the hieratic, masked, augmented stature and personal anonymity of the actors, who despite a given role like Oedipus or Pentheus could always symbolically stand in for the suffering Dionysus.

These relations point to the crucial subject of identification (III, 2). Greek tragedy may have died when the significance of the chorus was lost and the special, emotional interplay between audience, chorus, and action compromised. But identification still leads us into the action and, from our side, dissolves the Fourth Wall. We identify with our heroes and heroines. If they are too unlike ourselves, even evil, we can empathize, perhaps even sympathize, whether we are speaking of Richard in *Richard III* in Ian Mckellen's vivid screen enactment, or of Keaton, a bad, reformed cop going bad again, or Verbal, the devil incarnate, both in *The Usual Suspects*. After seeing what ordinary people are capable of in this century, we are aware that these characters all speak to elements within ourselves. Any character, conceived of with enough force and interest, will generate our fascination and win our belief, for we start every story hungry to believe.

This leads to a deceptively simple question. Put to one side all that has been and will be said about film, film technology, dramatic structure, historical sources, birth, rebirth, underlying psychic concerns and instinctual pleasures, or what we have seen the basic story pattern to be.

Where do stories happen?

In our minds.

A story that happens only on the screen does not happen at all. It stands apart from us, without integration into our feelings. Through the forms of identification and our instinct to believe, the story happens in us, or it does not happen at all.

The fundamental story pattern is the pattern of our attending that makes sense of our experience.

A screenwriter uses our instinctual belief and identifications to lead us into a vicarious experience of an action that makes the unknown known, resolves the unresolved, and creates meaning in place of incomprehension. This is a visionary process (VI). Along the way we are entertained, educated, delighted by representation, permitted pure entertainment to the point of escapism, and given a vicarious sense of mastered experience, which makes a story complete as well as completed. The elements of dramatic structure are the specific means by which our reason and emotions are shaped to a screenwriter's vision, for a story without such a shaping vision is one of meaningless incident that no one can believe or feel.

II   Primary Plot Elements

1. Screenplay Defined

Short form: A screenplay is a filmed, enacted, immediate, sequential symbolic imitation of an action with a complete Beginning, Middle, and End that falls within the larger fundamental story pattern, possessing an inherent significance, generated by the action of characters attempting to and ultimately resolving conflict-generating problems, whose outcome embodies the vision of the screenwriter, whose purpose is to please, divert, illumine, master, and resolve crucial innate drives in each audience member.

Complete form: A screenplay is a story that falls naturally within the fundamental story pattern that we experience as immediate, enacted, sequential, and filmed. The immediate surface is largely an imitation of an action, which is a movement of emotion and thought excited and guided in the individual viewer through a screenwriter's choice and treatment of character and incident in an action guided by the story structure, or plot. That action is always generated by immediate problems that the characters must solve and eventually do, for better or worse. Since drama imitates imagined lives, and life is a series of temporal actions, drama creates the illusion of representative, symbolic actions that we call the "imitation of an action." Life is not what is seen on screen or stage: what is seen is only these imagined moments able to stand for larger sequences of living. In this way years can be encompassed in minutes.

The goal of a screenplay is to entertain, to educate through the reflections rising from the action, to provide escape from the boredom of everyday existence, and to redeem its suffering by illusion, to create a sense of mastery over experience and comprehension of its meaning and, at its simplest, to give pleasure through delight in its various representative illusions.

Underlying the immediate action are essential social and psychic uses and conciliations involving order and disorder, ignorance and knowledge, passion and balance, reality and illusion (I). There is, further, an instinctual base in our delight in imitation, rhythm, will to believe, and mythopoetic drive. The resolution of the conflict at the end of the action is a conciliation of innate splits within ourselves (II, 3).

The imitation of the action may range from seeming realism to worlds of symbol and fantasy. The screenplay is an engine of transformation, linking and resolving past and present difficulties, enlightening its characters as they struggle to resolve their problems, and hence enlightening us, ultimately achieving a sense of unity, wholeness, closure, and a new beginning.

All plots, in all styles, have a Beginning, Middle, and End; a Crisis at the end of the Middle; and a Climax, wherein all is resolved and made known. Plots commonly contain one or more subplots, parallel or not. The material suitable for dramatic treatment within the fundamental story pattern falls into such a structure, and best echoes the reality it seeks to imitate. As screenplays are individual and unique, both the fundamental story pattern and the Beginning, Middle, and End structure it contains are subject to almost infinite variation.

If it were not so, anyone with a book of "rules" could become a good dramatist. Nothing is farther from the truth.

The choice of incidents is governed by the stylistic intention of a screenwriter and, fundamentally, by his informing vision, which he realizes and communicates through the action in which his vision and the thematic material contained in that must be implicit. The incidents are experienced with a sense of accumulating moral urgency (VI, 4). The physical means of viewing screenplays automatically lends them a sense of significance; their duration usually extends toward two hours (I, 4).

The incidents of the action must be consistent, coherent, and progressive: we must feel an accelerating rhythm, unconsciously musical, as the action moves toward its defining and resolving moments. The incidents must show an immediate cause-and-effect sequence of behavior and motivation. The action *is* that immediate flow of characters in conflict: all other story elements are experienced through the behavior of these characters. Dramatic elements must be at least necessary and probable within the premise of a given story, no matter how far removed from realism, while for a screenplay to earn our accolade as a good piece of dramatic writing, *all* elements from the premise to the concluding incident must seem necessary and probable.

We engage through the forms of identification with the main characters to whom a screenwriter gives an illusory force of existence. A screenplay compromises our commitment to believe at its peril. The immense technology that makes such stories possible must remain transparent through their actual enjoyment. A screenplay will be ineffective to the extent that any of these elements are lacking.

Experiencing a screenplay remains social and communal: it is at once an individual and a mass phenomenon, which fills our lives and on which we spend, worldwide, countless billions of dollars.[17]

2. Where Stories Come From

Why one story but not another sets a writer on fire is a mystery. A story can come from anywhere, from a newspaper or magazine article, or a news broadcast; from myth, the Bible, history, biography, autobiography, anthropology, or other stories, including those from the stage, television, or screen that inspire a writer to a fresh variant. Or a screenwriter may overhear others talking of some professional or private problem, encounter some outrageous or altruistic behavior, and be motivated to write.

He may be inspired to write one of the adaptations from novels common to film and eligible for one of the writing Oscars. He may be caught up in a daydream and suddenly *have* to develop that into a coherent story structure as the mythopoetic drive in the mind finds meat to its liking. A story may rise directly from a dream, or start from a half-awake twilight state inhabited by characters who *insist* that we find a home for *them* in a story.

A screenwriter may pursue an idea that a friend lets go, or a story may represent the means to distance and resolve elements of his own history and conflicts. Any story will tie in with a screenwriter's innermost conflicts and experiences in some manner, or it would not occur to him that this story as opposed to another is worth telling, even if the screenwriter thinks he is developing only a commercial, imitative variant of a current fad.

New writers seek material that they think will be desirable and write it in ways that they have been told are proper. Invariably, such an approach produces poor scripts. Good screenwriters or directors always urge novices to write the story that generates their greatest commitment, work, and insight, whatever it may be. That story may have the quality of excitement and the original force needed to make an impression and sell. Stories written by prescription feel like they are written by prescription and are almost always pallid imitations of the real thing.

Writers get nowhere if they self-consciously try to use the elements in chapter I. In a good dramatic story the critical elements emerge naturally and can then be sharpened in revision. The writer who starts trying to be his or her own philosopher, critic, aesthetician, anthropologist, archaeologist, and psychoanalyst guarantees that Page 1 stays blank.

Stories may well up in us from sources we never fathom. Once present, it is the story that a screenwriter must attend to, not his preconceptions. Every screenwriter has had the experience of being led on a road of discovery by her own characters as a story comes to life. The idea of a muse grows from this experience, for all the hard work we do in thinking through plot, character, and theme. Lonely as it may be, a screenwriter must trust to his own genius. If asked to define screenwriting, he must be able to answer: "It is what I write."

3. The Nature of Conflict

"Drama" and "conflict" are synonyms.

Conflict is innate, growing out of the tragic nature of our existence: we can never know all there is to know, never hold on to love despite all our efforts, for we must surrender and pass from the scene, however ardently we yearn for immortality. Very likely, the sole attribute that wholly separates us from the animals is our consciousness of this dilemma.

Worse, those who have eaten of the tree of knowledge cannot remain in the garden. We always live with an innate sense of loss, a boundless desire to undo or, failing that, deny or transcend our lost, unconscious unity with nature. Our dramas have always catered to that hunger through their usual "live happily ever after, after all conflicts are resolved" endings. Aristotle lamented the popularity of such dramas: they remain typical today because they accord with this deep desire. Underlying all our dramas is this "rite of reconciliation."

Drama is the means by which this innate condition is immediately, if symbolically, expressed and momentarily resolved.

Dramatic conflict is not the same as argument or daily conflict. In reality, issues can stay unresolved through a lifetime of argument. *But dramatic conflict arises from a problem that must be resolved one way or another and always is.* Dramatic conflict is structured into a clear *beginning, middle,* and *end:* it is immediately established, developed, resolved, and understood. Life is rarely so defined and feels traumatic when it is. The dramatic imitation of an action, then, is the imitation of a rare conflict, one in which conflict is developed in a structurally confined and coherent way to achieve resolution and significance.

One of the first questions we ask as a story starts is, What keeps everyone wherever they are? It is a problem that they must solve, but which resists solution; otherwise, the story would end immediately. Verbal, in *The Usual Suspects,* has made a deal and wants to leave, but

Detective Kujan holds him, forcing him to explain the truth behind the story he used to gain his deal. The film that follows results from their conflict.

Conflict is this collision of opposing wills. That collision is between characters, between a character and some impersonal force or obstacle, or between desires within the character himself. Jeff has to persuade Lisa that a murder has been committed in *Rear Window*. James Bond must climb a cliff that *leans outward* and is heavily guarded in *For Your Eyes Only*. Or a character must survive an earthquake, a hurricane, a volcano, or . . . Michael is torn by opposing desires to stay out of the family business and to help his father in *The Godfather*. There is always an *obstacle* to the hero's attempt to solve the problem that is innate to the problem or provided by his own opposing desires or those of other characters. His or her intention is always to overcome the problem or obstacle and live in a state of peace.

Effective conflict is defined: it always results from a specific attempt in response to a specific problem or obstacle to seek a specific solution. The more a screenwriter defines all his elements, the more material his imagination has to work with. The indefinite is a blur.

A conflict is experienced moment by moment, and always has something *specifically at stake:* to leave, or not to leave; to shoot, or not to shoot; to kiss, or not to kiss.

A conflict always has something *ultimately at stake.* Michael in the war council in *The Godfather* immediately wants his plan to avenge the assassination attempt on his father taken seriously, but riding on the outcome of that desire is the issue of who really understands what should be done for the family and is the true heir. Ted immediately wants to stop Joanna from going out the door in *Kramer vs. Kramer,* but her departure carries with it the larger issue of the failure of a marriage and the question of whether Ted can function successfully as both father and mother.

Thus conflict arises from a problem, involves a collision of wills or of a will and an opposing obstacle, is utterly specific, and has, scene by scene, an immediate and ultimate bearing on the outcome and meaning of the story.

But what is finally at stake in a conflict is always in some sense the survival of the hero or heroine. This is often understood literally: can Book, in *Witness*, as well as Rachel and Samuel, live? Can Kane, in *High Noon*, survive? Can Bill Munny survive the final shootout in *Unforgiven*? Can Jeff survive the salesman's attack in *Rear Window*? Can Michael and his family survive in *The Godfather* (any version)? Will the female tyrannosaur in *Jurassic Park: The Lost World* be killed in the process of regaining her child?

Survival also may be understood existentially, but nonetheless crucially. Is Charlie, in *Roxanne*, condemned forever to life as a freak, or is there a chance for him to have a real life, with love and meaning? Can Blanche, in *A Streetcar Named Desire*, find a new life, a second chance, wholeness and healing, or will she too be swept away? Will Scarlett, in *Gone With the Wind*, be able to carry on and build a new life, or will she be crushed by her mistakes and Rhett's abandonment? Can the family of Ted and Billy survive in *Kramer vs. Kramer*, or is it to be destroyed? Can Alexander survive, or will he be spiritually killed by Bishop Vergerus in *Fanny and Alexander*? Is Julie in *Blue* condemned to a living death, or can she find her way back to love and generation?

Each character finds his or her life or what matters most to him or her at stake, and so, too, does the audience living vicariously through them.

Good writing has life-and-death importance.

4. Location, Scene, Sequence

The conflict in screenplays occurs in locations, scenes, and sequences. A location is a specific, single site at which some fragment of the action takes place: everything in a film happens at one location or another. A location may be part of a larger sequence of locations, provide an element of visualization needed for continuity, prepare us for a fresh complication in the action, or provide a single piece of symbolic action.

We watch a car chase begin in an alley, move to a residential street, then to a freeway, down an off-ramp onto a surface street, race up a hill, fly off its crest, and so on until it is ended by a climactic capture or escape. Each of these specific sites is a location where some part of the chase is filmed.

We may see a plane in flight as part of an action's physical continuity: in *Prizzi's Honor*, for example, repetitive shots of a plane going back and forth give a humorous, visual form to the hit man's divided loyalties.

Or we know Joanna has returned when we see her through a coffee shop window late in *Kramer vs. Kramer*. This drives the action forward: shortly afterward, she contacts Ted and begins her effort to reclaim her son.

Julie, in *Blue*, rubs her knuckles along a stone wall, drawing blood. The action shown in that location is symbolic: Julie has closed herself off to grief and can only feel pain sensuously.

A *scene* is the smallest piece of the dramatic action on the part of the protagonists in response to an immediate problem that contains a complete beginning, middle, and end.

Ben's seduction by Mrs. Robinson in *The Graduate* occurs in one location, a hotel room. Ben joins Mrs. Robinson: she begins to strip, and Ben calls a halt, explaining he can't do this (beginning). He now makes an effort to find something else for them to do, which collapses when Mrs. Robinson challenges his masculinity (middle). Stung, Ben loses his temper and stays to prove his adequacy (end). A problem appears needing to be solved (a seduction attempt), an effort to solve it is made (Ben's futile effort to divert Mrs. Robinson), followed by a final effort at resolution (Ben's outraged assertion of masculinity, permitting the seduction to go forward).

This is the fundamental pattern of action in a scene, within the Beginning, Middle, and End segments of a screenplay, and of a screenplay itself.

Several locations are involved for the scene where Lucille, in *Blue*, summons Julie: the action moves from a phone call that Julie receives in her apartment to several different locations at the club where Lucille works. Only one beginning, middle, and end occurs. When Alexander is forced by Ismael to embody his hatred of Bishop Vergerus in *Fanny and Alexander*, the action of the scene moves back and forth between Ismael's room and various locations in the Bishop's palace.

Love scenes are often tritely split among several locations. A scene may start as one character joins another, continue through a candlelit dinner, move to a stroll in a park or along a romantic stretch of river, and climax in bed.

A *sequence* is a major part of a screenplay's action containing extended multiple locations and/or scenes, with its own beginning, middle, and end, organized around a single objective on the part of the hero or heroine, and set off in response to a specific problem: to get the stolen Ark *(Raiders of the Lost Ark)*, to get one's rights *(On the Waterfront)*, to catch an escaping criminal *(Rear Window)*. A scene set in multiple locations feels like a mini-sequence, and so creates a gray area for definition, although the difference between a scene and sequence is clear in practice.

The truck-fight episode in *Raiders of the Lost Ark* is a sequence made up of multiple locations, as are most action sequences, including car chases. Indiana Jones, on horseback, catches up with the truck carrying the stolen Ark, fights for control in the cab as they drive through several locations, wins, is wounded, loses control, falls on the road behind the truck, pulls himself back onto the truck with his whip, climbs along the truck and swings back into the cab, again wins control, pursues the car ahead of him, and finally pushes it off the road and escapes. In the beginning he must reach the truck and take control; in the middle he must maintain control against repeated efforts to dislodge him, until at the crisis he is ejected; at the end, he climactically regains control and succeeds in keeping the Ark.

When Terry goes down to the docks "to get my rights" in *On the Waterfront*, we encounter a sequence made up of multiple scenes. First, he must confront Edie, who wants him to flee, in the apartment; then he encounters Big Mac, who won't hire him, by the warehouse;

and then he confronts Johnny Friendly by his dockside office, first verbally, then physically. Finally Terry must be persuaded to get to his feet and lead the workers into the warehouse. Each of these scenes is clearly subordinated to a particular line of action.

The number of sequences will vary in screenplays, but the action within scenes and sequences should always have something immediately and ultimately at stake. A mere fragment of action in a single location has less weight.

5. Starting Stories: Establishing Character and Conflict

Every element of a screenplay is crucial, given the brevity and great ambition of the genre. The beginning part of the Beginning establishes the time, location, character(s), and immediate problem-generating conflict of the action. We are swiftly oriented to the style of a given story, from realism to fantasy, which must remain consistent. The beginning satisfies those urgent questions that we ask when trying to ground ourselves in the story: where are we, who is there, why are they there, what are they doing, what is the problem, why can't it be easily solved, what do they try to do?

Sometimes a story starts with a bang, as when Darth Vader's ship pursues Princess Leia's at the start of *Star Wars,* or when rows of bodies line a dock beside a burning ship, as in *The Usual Suspects;* a cowboy slices a woman's face at the start of *Unforgiven,* while *Jurassic Park* starts with a worker being caught and eaten by a velociraptor.

Or a screenwriter may start gradually, as when the camera pans the apartments visible from Jeff's window in *Rear Window* and finally focuses on him in his room, hot, bored, with a leg in a cast. Nothing more dramatic happens than the arrival of his nurse and dialogue that prepares the ground for his relationship with Lisa. *Schindler's List* starts with seder candles, then shows Schindler dressing and going to a restaurant, where he fetes the Nazi officers whose help he wants. In *Shane,* the title character rides up to the farm and accepts work as a farmhand.

It doesn't matter whether a story starts straightforwardly *(High*

Noon), with major flashbacks *(Lawrence of Arabia, The Usual Suspects, Suddenly Last Summer)*, or narration *(A River Runs Through It, The Usual Suspects)*.

No particular page length is mandated for the beginning section (or for any other). *Witness* opens with an extended, evocatory sequence of the funeral of Rachel's husband and typical farming sights of the Amish countryside. Rachel and Samuel must travel to Baltimore and be delayed in Philadelphia before Samuel witnesses the key murder. Only then does Book enter the action. *The Godfather* takes us through a marriage party with interwoven scenes in the don's office, the parking lot, an upstairs room where Sonny is having an affair, and a corner of the garden where Kay and Michael sit watching the action. A subsequent sequence centered on getting a starring role for Johnny in Hollywood follows before the main action starts.

There is no "better" way: the choice must fit the particular story to be told, influenced by the genius of a writer and the length appropriate to the circumstances of the story.

In Kantian terms we establish the space (setting), the causality (the why and wherefore), and the time frame. In Nietzschean we elaborate the first illusions from which the illusion of the action develops. From the point of view of innate creativity, expressed as play, we define our game, as do children in their precursors to drama when they decide who will be the Mommy, who the Daddy; who the Robber, who the Cop; who the Indian, who the Cowboy; who the Nurse, who the Doctor, and what problem they will deal with, according to what rules.

6. Starting Stories: Choosing Material and Treatment

How do we know what material belongs in a story in the first place, and how to portray it?

The screenwriter must know, or develop and clarify through revision, a premise for the story, which is a capsule conception of two main points: the action's essential problem(s) and the point of the story, or vision, as driven home in the Climax. Action that contributes to the realization of that vision is relevant and should be written from the perspective implied; anything else is dispensable, or mishandled. Discovering these elements through trial and error is common: stories do not spring full-blown from the imagination. This is as true for stories written on speculation as for those commissioned and developed through a formal premise (or idea or presentation) and treatment (VIII, 2). The effort to form this premise for conflict and vision is crucial to the success of the story.

A premise for *Witness* might run: "A young Amish boy witnesses a murder that leads to the exposure of police corruption and a romance between the investigating officer and the boy's recently widowed mother, but since old-fashioned yet enviable Amish values can no longer mix with the modern, violent world, the officer leaves the mother behind among the Amish at the end even though he succeeds in overcoming the corrupt police."

Now we know to establish the Amish boy and his mother, which involves establishing the Amish, and her loss, before moving to the murder and the ensuing action that involves the romance between Rachel and Book. But because we also know the point of the story, which is a story about values, we know how to portray the material. Amish material will be shown in a largely favorable light, the "English," as the Amish refer to us generically, in a largely unfavorable one.

A premise for *Hamlet* might run: "The ghost of Hamlet's father returns to demand vengeance on his brother, whom he claims murdered him, usurped his crown, and married his wife. Hamlet isn't sure that the ghost can be trusted, and he has seen so deeply into the nature of reality that he believes action is an illusion, and so Hamlet is reduced to drift, taking advantage of circumstances, yet unable to act decisively except in moments of passion."

This gives us an essential grasp of the key problem in Hamlet and the vision or point of view from which to build the action and climax. We would know to establish Hamlet's world through the appearance of the ghost in medieval Elsinore and the problem through the ghost's demand and Hamlet's ambivalence. Thereafter Hamlet must seek to prove the king's guilt, yet never be convinced by his efforts or, convinced, be able to act until driven by spontaneous rage at the conclusion.

The premise for Kurosawa's *Kagemusha* is this: "A thief is utilized as a stand-in for Shingen, a great warlord, because of their uncanny resemblance. The thief continues the impersonation after Shingen's death to defer the day of reckoning for the clan. He is able to deceive all, but identifying with the late Shingen, he exposes himself by futilely trying to ride a horse that only the warlord could master. Publicly exposed, the thief is cast out, the death of Shingen revealed, and the thief and the clan destroyed." Fate is unavoidable.

Given such a premise, we need then to establish the clan, the death of the warlord, and the crucial utility of the look-alike—but because we know his end is tragic, and caused by mistaken pride, from the beginning we will show his look-alike endangered both by those whom he must deceive in order to save, and by himself as he confuses identities. At the end, as in *Hamlet,* all will have been for nothing.

7. Backstory, Preparation, and Exposition

Backstory creates and contains all those considerable story elements that typically precede the immediate dramatic action in the fundamental story pattern, including the past lives of the characters, their development, unknown or lingering problems, and the screenwriter's perspective on the material (I, 1). A screenwriter may invent more material than he finally needs, though all helps him to define his characters and their problems and his own vision.

All crucial elements must be revealed, developed, and resolved within the immediate action. A screenwriter cannot imagine or begin his action without the context provided by the backstory (IV, 1). Although much backstory inevitably is developed through revision, a screenwriter must develop enough in advance to form a provisional, working premise (II, 6; VIII, 1–2).

Police corruption is backstory in *Witness,* and the different values of the Amish and the "English." Julie's indirect use of her musical genius as well as Patrice's extramarital affair are backstory in *Blue*. Kane's mistress is backstory in *High Noon*, the past imprisonment of the returning outlaw, and Kane's crucial sense of duty. All of Don Corleone's rise is backstory in *The Godfather*, and Michael's doomed intention to go straight. The Mongol conquest, German aggression, and Prince Alexander's practical patriotism are backstory in *Alexander Nevsky*; the abuse of sailors by officers and recent defeat are backstory in *The Battleship Potemkin*. The development of dinosaur DNA and the hubris of meddling with nature are backstory in *Jurassic Park*.

Preparation refers to props, events, or elements of behavior in the immediate action that lay the groundwork for future action. It is a continuous element. All beginnings prepare us for the ensuing action, and that, in turn, for later action. In *Witness*, the impact that Rachel makes on Book at lunch while still being detained in Philadelphia, as well as the quality of her nursing after he is wounded, prepare us for their later romance. McFee's wounding of Book prepares us for Book's flight and necessitates Rachel's nursing. Obi-Wan Kenobi's display of a Jedi's weapon to Luke at their first meeting establishes that weapon and prepares us for its later use, including Luke's training to become a Jedi Knight, in *Star Wars*.

Preparation reinforces our sense of the cause-and-effect pattern of the action, of things "adding up," a crucial part of maintaining credibility and fulfilling drama's larger role.

New or ineffective writers often have characters behave in unprepared ways or produce props, like guns, that we have no prior reason to expect a character to have or to know how to use. Shane convinces at the Climax of *Shane* because his past ability as a gunfighter is established earlier. Weak writers tend to substitute coincidence for preparation, damaging a story's inner coherence.

Properly prepared action retains its sense of surprise.

Much prepares us to discover the deception that Verbal practices on Kujan in *The Usual Suspects*, yet its climactic revelation as Kujan adds up the pieces literally before his eyes on the bulletin board is a brilliant surprise. It is one thing to see Obi-Wan Kenobi show Luke the light saber, another to see him slice off an arm. Book's discovery that McFee is the murderer in *Witness* prepares us for other police corruption; Captain Schaefer's involvement "fits," yet comes as a surprise.

Exposition is information necessary to characters to move the immediate action forward. Weak writers have characters offer it when an author's need arises; good writers motivate its delivery by characters in response to their immediate need. The Alliance's desperate, immediate need to destroy the Death Star motivates the explanation of its design in *Star Wars* after R2-D2's plans are delivered. Book explains the past disappearance of drugs and his connection of that to McFee in order to get Captain Schaefer's help in *Witness*. Marlowe delivers exposition at the Climax of *The Big Sleep* in order to convince Eddie Mars that he has finally figured him out: that, and Marlowe's threat to shoot him, drives Mars out of Geiger's house, where his own men shoot him instead. Michael's explanations of various people to Kay during the opening wedding sequence in *The Godfather* may be convenient for us as audience, but it is also information that Kay wants.

8. Complication, Major Reverse, Minor Reverse

A screenplay's action is driven forward by complications. "Complication" is the technical term for a dramatic problem. All screenplays start with a complication; each complication generates action and conflict; each requires multiple scenes or at least one sequence for its resolution. Some pose the fundamental problem that a screenplay must resolve, developed in turn by subsequent complications (II, 11–13). The resolution of all complications and the conflict they generate is the goal of the hero and heroine.

Witness starts with the complication of Rachel's widowhood. This motivates her to visit her sister in Baltimore to avoid familiar and evocative settings. When their connecting train is delayed in Philadelphia (another complication), Samuel witnesses a murder, the complication that entwines Book's and Rachel's fates and whose solution encompasses the screenplay.

Julie's husband and daughter are killed in an accident in the initial complication of *Blue*. Julie tries to commit suicide in the hospital, but can't. Although this second, major complication forces her to live, she does so by repressing her feelings and her past. Subsequent complications drive the action forward by challenging that repression: her simultaneous discovery that Olivier is completing a composition of her husband's and that her husband had a mistress is the complication that ultimately leads Julie to turn to Olivier for renewed life and love.

Major Reverses, referred to simply as Reverses, are sudden 180-degree turns in a major character's fortune, and as such are staples of dramatic writing. Reverses are usually complications: they can appear at any time in any kind of story. The Crisis at the end of a screenplay's Middle always contains a Reverse.

Oedipus Rex has the most famous Reverse, as Oedipus goes from being a respected king to being an incestuous, patricidal figure in only moments during the Crisis. *Kramer vs. Kramer* starts with a Reverse as Ted comes home after one of the best days of his life at work only to have his wife abandon him and their young son. Book undergoes a Reverse at the end of the Beginning of *Witness* when he discovers that McFee and Schaefer are both corrupt. Michael, in *Tootsie*'s Crisis, reveals himself to be a man in order to escape the intolerable consequences of impersonating a woman, a Reverse that affects him as an actress, actor, man, woman, friend, and lover. In a rare use of a Reverse to end the action, Detective Kujan in *The Usual Suspects* discovers moments after he lets Verbal go that Verbal, far from being a weakling and a cripple, is "the devil incarnate."

Reverses may appear with or without full recognition or discovery of their consequences by the characters. Oedipus and Book recognize what their Reverses mean; Ted refuses to see the implications of his. A Reverse with discovery is a particularly potent moment, especially when preparation makes it both inevitable and surprising.

The smallest unit into which the action can be broken is a minor reverse, referred to as a reverse with a small *r*. A reverse is a single exchange of action-reaction within a scene or sequence. A synonym used casually for minor reverse is "beat." Everything in a scene except the final reverse is a thwarting of the protagonist's immediate goal, forcing him to make a new effort to get his way and often changing the nature of his goal, as with Ben in the seduction scene from *The Graduate*.

Such reverses may coincide with a scene's beginning, middle, and end, as in that scene from *The Graduate*. In *Fanny and Alexander*, there are nine minor reverses in the confrontation between Alexander and Bishop Vergerus over Alexander's story concerning the death of the Bishop's previous wife and children. In *The Godfather* there are four as Michael persuades his brothers in the war council scene to let him kill McCluskey and Sollozzo; the last consists of Sonny's laughing dismissal of Michael and Michael's convincing comeback (action-reaction, or reverse: here Michael gets his way).

Quality isn't directly related to the number of minor reverses: the three-reverse seduction scene in *The Graduate* is amusing and sharp, the four-reverse war council in *The Godfather* effective. The latter is rich with implication despite its brevity concerning who truly understands what is "business" and what must be done. Many reverses in a scene may only indicate bloated writing.

Yet the confrontation scene between Alexander and Bishop Vergerus undoubtedly cuts more deeply than these simpler scenes. Alexander first seeks to avoid the consequences of his story by claiming that the maid Justine is lying. He fails, and is forced to take an oath he is telling the truth, considerably raising the stakes. Alexander uses the oath to try and leave, but is stopped by the Bishop. Now Alexander is driven to admit that he thinks the Bishop hates him, though Vergerus insists that he loves Alexander. Vergerus claims that his greater spiritual strength will triumph. But his triumph is only physical and costs the Bishop all moral ascendancy, for Alexander's will crumbles before a list of physical punishments, evidently some used against the Bishop when he was a child. Alexander confesses to lying and is beaten. When Alexander says he will "never" ask forgiveness, fighting to maintain some spark of self-respect and independence, a threat of more caning makes him do so. Alexander thinks he can at last get away, but in a final twist, he is locked in a dark attic.

The action of characters determined to get their way through extended minor reverses is enriched by elements of backstory. Characterization is deepened, and the sense of what is immediately and ultimately at stake is raised. This enrichment and deepening typifies Oedipus's confrontation with Teiresias in *Oedipus Rex*, Agave's recognition of her dead son in Euripides's *The Bacchae*, the bedroom scene between Hamlet and his mother in *Hamlet*, and the confrontations between Mitch and Blanche in *A Streetcar Named Desire*, Michael and Kaye in *The Godfather, Part II* when she reveals her abortion, and why, and between Charley and Terry in the taxi in *On the Waterfront*.

A screenwriter drives his imagination to find the wellsprings of character, conflict, and motivation through extended minor reverses within a scene. But all elements of a screenplay are encountered on the level of such minor reverses, whether complications, Reverses, discoveries, characters, or anything else. Such minor reverses constitute the immediate action that we, the audience, encounter.

The best writing always has a sense of disaster just barely avoided, minor reverse-by-reverse: it is always on the edge. One slip, and the villain gets Bond, Mitch leaves Blanche, Joanna goes out the door, or Kaye leaves Michael and takes the children.

9. Discovery and Its Types

Discoveries are different ways that characters gain insight and knowledge into themselves and the action.[18] A discovery is usually a surprise; combined with a Reverse, it is a powerful dramatic tool (II, 8). "Recognition" and "discovery" are interchangeable terms.

A discovery is often made through a sign: Charlie is known by his nose in *Roxanne;* tattooing reveals a true contender for the throne in *King Solomon's Mines*. A good deal turns on a cut and a tattoo in *Suspect*. The thief is exposed after his fall in *Kagemusha* because he lacks Shingen's scar.

Tokens are signs that prove a character's identity or achievement, like a detective's badge, or a feather, as in *The Four Feathers*. A tie links

Inspector Wes Block psychically with the killer in *Tightrope*. That killer's sneakers expose his disguise as a policeman. A special beer bottle reveals Dick as a murderer in *Waterland*.

Letters and overheard messages or phone calls are frequent discoveries by sign. Addresses recovered by tracing their outline on note pads are another. Samuel recognizes the killer from a photograph in a display case in *Witness*. Billy knows Guy and Jill have risked the curfew when he finds bullet holes in Guy's car in *The Year of Living Dangerously*.

Properly motivated exposition can create a discovery, while the same technique used merely at the author's convenience remains a fault here as well. Both occur in *Waterland*. Tom must explain who various people are when he takes his students on a class trip into time, but his climactic recitation at a school convocation is forced by the author, and forfeits belief. Jack the Ripper effectively tries to convince H. G. Wells that he fits into the twentieth century in *Time After Time* by showing him the violence on television.

Discovery through memory is endemic in screenwriting whether in psychoanalytic form as in *Suddenly Last Summer* or *The Prince of Tides*, or more generally as in *A River Runs Through It* as a quest for understanding. Memory can be regained after a trauma, coma, or amnesia. A character may simply resist remembering, because memory is inconvenient or painful, until driven to do so. A song can be associated with a key memory, as is the Varsouviana Waltz in Blanche's mind in *A Streetcar Named Desire*. The pressure of memory is overpowering in *Out of Africa*, as Karen recounts the loss of her Eden, and love. Tom exorcises his ghosts in *Waterland* and simultaneously shows his high school class the relevance of history.

Reasoning and false reasoning are commonplaces, especially in crime films. Kujan falsely reasons himself to a complete misunderstanding of Keaton and Verbal in *The Usual Suspects*. Book, on the other hand, correctly reasons from Samuel's discovery of the killer in *Witness* that there is corruption among the police; he just doesn't know that the captain is part of it.

- -

When Book discovers the full truth, it is through McFee's assassination attempt. This is a discovery through action. Hamlet learns through the king's reaction to the play-within-a-play that he is guilty. Henrietta discovers at the altar in *Four Weddings and a Funeral* that Charles loves another woman. Miss Kenton discovers that her husband is dependent and her daughter pregnant at the end of *The Remains of the Day;* consequently she parts from Mr. Stevens without admitting or acting on her love. Discovery through action turns on charged, emotional confrontations and has the greatest impact.

More broadly, characters are *surprised* by discovery and motivated to act, often in unexpected ways. Discovery and revelation are complementary: major revelations are also discoveries. A sense of discovery in good writing is continuous: Luke, Han, and company constantly discover themselves in new circumstances and dangers in *Star Wars.* Price and his classmates constantly discover new things in *Waterland,* while Tom tries to understand what has really happened to him.

A screenplay is always a voyage of discovery.

10. The Dramatic Obstacle, Change, and Suspense

A character encounters the immediate dramatic problem in a scene or sequence as a dramatic obstacle. The dramatic obstacle changes minor reverse by minor reverse; as it does so, what is immediately at stake in a scene or sequence alters. What is ultimately at stake is clarified by this movement of the action.

Ada is passionate but mute and expresses herself through her piano in *The Piano;* her husband sells it to Baines for land and insists that she give him lessons. Ada wants and needs her piano; reluctantly, she consents to give lessons in order to have its use. In a key scene she first requires her daughter to remain outside, then goes in to teach. But Baines just wants to listen to her play. As she does, he kisses her. Shocked, she stops. He offers a deal: she can regain ownership of the all-important piano by trading intimacies for a certain number of piano keys. Ada hesitates, but she wants the piano too badly not to bargain and finally agrees to a ratio of keys to intimacies. She doesn't intend the agreement to lead to profound intimacy. She resumes playing.

Ada is forced into new and unexpected behaviors as each minor reverse changes the dramatic obstacle she faces. She is in a new situation at the end of the scene and has changed somewhat as a character. Each change, each new behavior, comes as a surprise, a discovery, or a revelation. Baines's true desires are all three to Ada, while she starts to discover how far she is prepared to go to regain her piano.

Moreover, as the dramatic obstacle alters, what is ultimately at stake in a scene clarifies. Ada's immediate intention is to give lessons to have access to the piano; what is immediately at stake shifts from giving a lesson to refusing an advance to making a deal exchanging intimacies for keys. That lets us see that what is ultimately riding on this scene is a real possibility of a compromising relationship with Baines, which would complicate Ada's marriage and affect her desire to have the piano in unknown ways.

Characters operate in the dark, reverse by reverse, discover their way, reveal capacity, and are surprised and changed as they adapt to the changes imposed by the immediate obstacle.

Change is continuous in effective writing.

But operating in the dark like this necessarily creates suspense as characters are startled into fresh action to find ever new ways of overcoming the dramatic obstacle. Major suspense concerns our fear for the survival of the main characters, whether literal or metaphorical (II, 3); minor suspense concerns our fears for the survival of secondary characters, or action where the survival of the main character is not in question.

Drama is not a science, but its elements do add up coherently.

11. The Beginning: Development of the Dramatic Problem

We are now in position to review the structure basic to all screenplay plots.

A plot falls into a Beginning, Middle, and End; its action is only part of the fundamental story pattern (I, 1). Usually considerable story elements exist before the Beginning as backstory, typically including an important unresolved problem or event, while the final resolution of the End intimates without exploring a new beginning where all previous problems are resolved. In a sense, in Aristotelian terms, we start in medias res, in the middle.

The Beginning starts by establishing the hero or heroine's immediate reality and character through conflict generated by an initial complication (II, 3; 5–6). If the initial complication is not the main problem, that problem soon develops. The appearance of the main problem sooner or later forces the characters to take account of a past underlying problem or event that they have been able to ignore but now discover they must solve as part of the immediate conflict. That discovery results from the developmental pattern of the complications in the Beginning. At the end of the Beginning the protagonists deliberately form, or are fortuitously driven by circumstances into, a plan of action to resolve their problem. This is the turning point that defines the end of the Beginning.

The early Amish scenes establish Rachel's character, situation and conflict in *Witness*. Rachel's widowhood is the immediate complication that drives her to seek relief with her sister. She is delayed in Philadelphia, a second complication, but Book doesn't appear until Samuel witnesses a murder, the major complication of the screenplay that ultimately will force the past into the immediate action. The main characters do not fully realize the implications of the main problem when it appears. Thus they undertake a series of mistaken actions for its solution, each time discovering through ensuing complications that the main problem is other and larger than they thought. Throughout these developments Book and Rachel are at cross-purposes. Samuel fails to identify any suspects (fourth complication) until he comes across McFee's photograph in a trophy case full of award-winning officers (fifth complication). Book rushes to Captain Schaefer: he thinks he can solve the disappearance of a major drug haul in the past through McFee's corruption. Schaefer assures himself that no one but he and Book know of Book's discoveries. McFee then wounds Book in the garage of his apartment before fleeing, revealing that Schaefer is part of the corruption (Reverse). Now Book understands the problem facing himself, Rachel, and Samuel. Uncertain whom to trust, their lives in immediate danger, he flees with Rachel and Samuel: the main characters are now joined in purpose. Where does he go? To the Amish, established at the start, where they will be hard to trace. Book's solution is to buy time to find the final solution.

End of the Beginning.

Jeff is confined to his apartment with a broken leg in *Rear Window* (first complication), nursed by Thelma and lovingly pampered by beautiful Lisa. Their situation, character, and conflict are established, including the appearance of one unresolved conflict from the past, Lisa's desire to have Jeff either settle down or take her with him on assignments (he is a photographer with a penchant for wild or dangerous places). He won't do either (second complication). Jeff witnesses events through his window that make him believe a murder has been committed (major problem), but he cannot convince Lisa or Thelma. The main characters are at cross-purposes, and none of them fully realizes the implications of the problem with regard to either the murder or how the resolution of the murder will lead to a resolution of Lisa and Jeff's underlying problem. Lisa's stream of reproaches against Jeff for peeping into others' lives and making wild accusations abruptly stops when she can see into the murdered woman's room. The wife, an invalid, has disappeared. Men are removing a trunk. Lisa now turns to Jeff and demands that he tell her what he thinks happened (Reverse), and how, indicating that they will now act together to solve the problem.

End of the Beginning.

Princess Leia, Darth Vader, and the war between the Alliance and the Empire are established in the beginning of *Star Wars* as Leia is captured (first complication). R2-D2 escapes with crucial information, but is captured and sold to Luke's family before reaching his destination (second complication). Now Luke is established, including his thwarted desire to escape his circumstances. R2-D2 escapes (third complication), Luke pursues, and is saved from death by Obi-Wan

Kenobi. R2-D2 now reveals Leia's crucial plea for Obi-Wan's help (main problem). Obi-Wan wants Luke to become a Jedi Knight like his father and to help him. Luke declines. The main characters are at cross-purposes, and none of them fully understands the implications of the main problem. Luke discovers a series of storm trooper murders that include his uncle and aunt. He cannot escape this fight (Reverse). He resolves to return R2-D2 to Aldaran with Obi-Wan Kenobi; they hire Han Solo to take them. Subplots have established Han's need for money and the destruction of Aldaran by the Death Star. Han, Luke, and Obi-Wan now think they understand the problem, which they do in part. Three of the four main characters are linked, have a plan, and blast off.

End of the Beginning.

The Beginning always ends with a turning point, a clarified, specific line of action that the main characters hope will solve the problem confronting them, which they now rightly believe they understand better. They still have a great deal more to discover, and their plan will prove adequate only after considerable modification or abandonment for a new one as a result of the Crisis at the end of the Middle. The Beginning always links the main characters after initial conflict if there are a hero and heroine or multiple sets of heroes. The line of action at its end leads inevitably into the Middle and focuses our attention in a particular direction. A Reverse need not be used at the end of the Beginning: *Blue* does not use one; neither does *On the Waterfront* or many other films.

Circumstances drive Book and Rachel to flight in *Witness*, while Luke and friends in *Star Wars*—and even more so Lisa and Jeff in *Rear Window*—choose their undertaking. Either is effective, and the choice depends on the nature of a given story. Moreover, the meaning of their choices may be clear to them, or they may require the help of later events to come to the surface, as with Julie in *Blue*, Terry in *On the Waterfront*, or Ichimonji in *Ran*.

The major turn in the action at the end of the Beginning may be a defined moment, as when Lisa stares across the courtyard into the empty bedroom and demands that Jeff tell her all he knows, or it may happen in a sequence. The turning point at the end of the Beginning in *Witness* can be understood as Book's flight with Samuel and Rachel; however, that flight is at the start of a sequence that ends when Book drops them off at their farm and crashes into the birdhouse, too wounded to leave.

The end of the Beginning in *Blue* is Julie's actual departure to the city, abandoning her past. But that departure is also part of a sequence that ends only after she is established in the city and refuses to sign a petition to get rid of Lucille, explaining that she, Julie, intends to be totally uninvolved.

The action is unfocused without this critical turning point at the end of the Beginning; the use of a defined moment to dramatize it has immediate impact, while the use of a sequence has a more "slice-of-life" realism to it. Each is effective.

Finally, the Beginning itself has a beginning, middle, and end. The beginning of *Witness* takes us through Book's holding Samuel and Rachel. The middle consists of Samuel's efforts to identify the killer; its crisis is identifying McFee. The end contains Book's betrayal by Schaefer and attack by McFee, and his climactic flight. This beginning-middle-end pattern exists through scenes, sequences, each part of the Beginning, Middle, and End segments of the screenplay, and for the entire screenplay. It is a key ingredient in giving a story its illusory coherence and persuasiveness, and is or has become our virtually instinctive way of telling dramatic stories.

12. The Middle: Development to the Crisis

In the Middle the protagonists follow through on the line of action they have chosen or have been driven into at the end of the Beginning to solve their problem. Their characters, relationships, and conflict develop significantly through the Middle's complications, as do any new characters. Their effort to resolve the conflict reaches the Crisis at the end of the Middle, where the protagonists' relationships and the resolve that has guided their action face collapse, or do collapse, endangering their survival.

At the end of the Beginning the thief in *Kagemusha* agrees to impersonate Shingen, although Shingen has died. The thief manages to deceive the dead warlord's wives and those retainers not among the select group making use of him. He handles a challenge in a council to pronounce policy, for which he has no background, and presides over a battle with "his" forces. "His" grandson comes to love him. The clan's opponents are baffled and remain inactive, unsure of the situation. But the thief finally starts to believe his own charade and tries to mount the horse that only Shingen could master. The thief is thrown, exposed, and banished: Crisis.

Karin wins her parents' consent to bring candles to the church at the end of the Beginning in Bergman's *The Virgin Spring* and sets off with a servant girl, Ingerli. Ingerli abandons her, and Karin foolhardily goes on alone. She meets robbers posing as shepherds in the woods and graciously shares her meal with them. Ingerli, hidden, watches. Karin then recognizes that the goats are her father's, while a frog that Ingerli hid in Karin's lunch is exposed in the food she is sharing. They attack, rape, and kill her: Crisis.

Munny, the Schofield Kid, and Ned, Munny's close friend, join forces at the end of the Beginning to kill the cowboys who slashed a whore's face in *Unforgiven*. When they reach Big Whiskey, Munny is beaten, then nursed to health by the slashed whore. He and the Kid kill the cowboys; Ned can't kill anymore, and leaves. The Kid discovers killing is horrible. Munny discovers as they are paid that Ned has been caught, tortured, and killed: Crisis.

Nikita is released from training at the end of the Beginning of *La Femme Nikita* and given a new identity and an apartment to use as a cover for her secret assignments. She tries to lead a normal life, falls in love with Marco, and tries to function as an agent. A disastrous assignment proves she can neither bear killing nor have a normal life: Crisis.

Hamlet plans to catch Claudius's conscience at the end of the Beginning in a play to be put on by the Players. First he rejects Ophelia, questions himself in the "To be, or not to be" soliloquy, and trains the Players to enact his father's murder. Claudius rushes away from the performance, overwhelmed with guilt. Hamlet, sure that Claudius is guilty, does not kill him at prayer, or after a traumatic scene with his mother; instead, he is packed off to England, first running into a captain of Fortinbras's, which lets him remark on the uselessness of political/military action. Claudius arranges for his assassination in England: Crisis.

Just as the turning point at the end of the Beginning focuses the action for the Middle, the Crisis narrows the action down even more, sometimes to a specific task. Nikita must find a way out; Munny must find vengeance for Ned, and Karin's father, for Karin: Alan and Ellie and the children must survive the velociraptors in *Jurassic Park*. Lisa and Jeff must find the killer on their own in *Rear Window*; Book has to confront the corrupt police in *Witness*, Dave must survive the monolith in *2001*, Keaton and his gang in *The Usual Suspects* have to carry through on the attack on the freighter.

The Middle's developmental pattern falls into its own beginning, middle, and end. Book is nourished to health in the beginning of the Middle in *Witness*. Recovered, he contacts his partner Carter to tell him he will stay away from Philadelphia until able to find a solution to Schaefer and McFee. Eli challenges him to help on the farm now that he is recovered, and Book agrees, starting with an early breakfast and milking. In the middle he and Rachel fall in love. Schaefer realizes that Book can't be traced among the Amish. Some Amish, like Daniel, who wants Rachel for himself, wonder when Book will leave. Eli warns Rachel she risks shunning because of Book. Rachel defiantly singles him out in a barn-raising sequence, but when she offers herself that night, Book declines: end of the middle of the Middle, with its own crisis. In the end of the Middle Book explains that accepting her offer would mean he must stay, or she must leave: Rachel is struck dumb. He gives himself away in an act of public violence in town when he learns his partner has been killed. That evening Rachel gives herself to him in the fields. At dawn Schaefer's car stops on the rise overlooking the farm: end of the Middle, its climax, and the Crisis.

The action often changes locale in the Middle. *Witness* moves from the city to an Amish community, *Blue* from Julie's home to the city, *Unforgiven* to Big Whiskey in Montana, *La Femme Nikita* from the training institute to the city, *The Virgin Spring* to the forest, *2001* to a spaceship bound for Jupiter, *Star Wars* to the Aldaran system and the Death Star.

Many stories do not change locales, like *A River Runs Through It*, *High Noon*, *Hamlet*, *Oedipus Rex*, *The Professional*, *Kramer vs. Kramer*, *The Piano*, *On the Waterfront*, and countless others. A change in locales is a helpful defining element, but not a necessary one; its presence depends on the needs of a given story.

New characters are often introduced, like the corrupt camp commander that the 54th Massachusetts Infantry encounters when sent south in *Glory*. Doyle appears and plays a key role in *Rear Window*. The robbers in *The Virgin Spring*, Nikita's lover in *La Femme Nikita*, Lucille in *Blue*, and the tyrannosaur in *Jurassic Park* all appear in the Middle. As important a character as Agave doesn't appear until the End in Euripides's *The Bacchae*.

Characters who have been only slightly utilized earlier often assume major roles in the Middle, as Leia in *Star Wars*, the various Amish in *Witness*, Gertrude in *Hamlet*, the president's wife in *Dave*, or Joanna in *Kramer vs. Kramer*. Whether new or slightly used earlier, such characters lend a fresh charge to the action in the Middle.

Finally, the Beginning is usually longer than the Middle, as it must introduce the main characters, define their reality, and initiate and develop the conflict. Sometimes each segment is roughly the same length, as in *Chinatown* or *Rear Window*. Sometimes the Middle predominates. A screenwriter should not look for a schema based on page numbers but for the structure that develops and fits his unique story.

13. The End: Climax and Resolution

The End, or Climax, is the concluding action taken by the protagonists in direct response to the Crisis. That reveals the ultimate dimension of the problem they must solve in the End, or lose all that matters to them. The characters' climactic efforts define their physical and spiritual capacity; the outcome of the their efforts reveals the ultimate meaning, or point, or vision that motivated the selection and treatment of the material from the start. All immediate and underlying problems from the past are resolved, revealed, and clarified. Sometimes a brief resolution follows the Climax to tie up loose ends or drive home the meaning of the Climax.

Ada's husband, Stewart, cuts off one of her fingers in the Crisis of *The Piano*. They cannot remain together; an attempt to rape her fails, and he goes to Baines and demands that he leave with Ada. Baines and Ada take the piano, but when it is thrown overboard on their journey, Ada steps into the hissing rope and is drawn underwater. There she could die into perfect silence, but she releases herself and lets the piano go. She discovers she loves Baines and through him, life. In a brief resolution we see her learning to speak again, undoing the burden of her past, and again playing, now with an artificial finger made by Baines.

The Crisis clearly sets the stage for this action, while the characters' choices are final and defining: Stewart lets go of a woman he cannot let "play" him; Baines, for Ada's sake, embarks on a settled life; she, from discovered love, chooses his companionship over private, abstract passion. Their actions clearly imply that to live we must love, and loving means to exist within a shared world.

Past and present are always reconciled in the End.

Terry's brother is killed and Terry's efforts to exercise choice determined by conscience are undone in the Crisis of *On the Waterfront*. Terry must confront Johnny Friendly and the corrupt union. Testifying against Friendly in court leaves Terry ostracized, and Edie wants him to run away. His confrontation must, then, be direct. Terry goes down to the docks "to get his rights." He prevails over Johnny Friendly, arguing over who understands the past best; although physically beaten, he gets to his feet and leads the longshoremen into work despite Johnny Friendly's helpless protests. He shows he has what it takes now.

This means that Terry's version of reality prevails, that Johnny was the bum—not Terry, that standing up for one's convictions is right, that the truth is a preeminent value, and that relationships based on falsehood or fear are lies to be swept away. Terry has become the true leader.

The Climax in *Witness* sees Book overcome the captain and the corrupt police, resolving the problem from the past. Book shows that he is tougher, luckier, and more ingenious than they. But in the resolution he leaves Samuel and Rachel behind. That outcome clearly drives home a vision of reality in which the worlds of the violent "English" and the peaceful and communal Amish are shown to represent irreconcilable value systems. "Love is not everything"; we are doomed to live corrupted lives, which is to say we need to change in major ways.

These choices are revelatory. They have been prepared for and feel inevitable once made (II, 7), yet come as surprises within a tense, suspenseful situation. Luke in *Star Wars* reveals that he has the making of a Jedi Knight by trusting to the Force to guide his lethal shot; Hamlet reveals that he can only act spontaneously as the discovery of his mother's, Laertes', and his own poisoning leads him finally to kill Claudius in a fit of passion. Karin's father reveals an inhuman rage when he kills even the young, guiltless boy along with his daughter's murderers in *The Virgin Spring*.

The pattern of resolution of immediate and past problems, revelation, and final clarity of the governing vision of a dramatic story in the End is universal in drama, and has existed from the start. Oedipus blinds himself and is banished at the End of *Oedipus Rex*, while Jocasta hangs herself. The immediate problems of incest and the plague afflicting Thebes are resolved, while Oedipus's past murder of his father is avenged, and the even older prophecy that he would kill his father and marry his mother is revealed to have been carried out by his own efforts to avoid it. Even wise men are sadly limited: one's fate cannot be avoided. All reaches a final definition and clarity.

The End may be relatively short, as in *Witness,* or in *Kramer vs. Kramer,* where after losing the trial, Ted swiftly decides not to appeal, prepares Billy to leave, and is reprieved by Joanna. It may be considerably extended, as in *The Piano, Hamlet,* or *On the Waterfront,* or even equal in length with the Middle, as in *Rear Window*. No particular page length should be artificially observed. It does not matter if one story requires a resolution separate from the Climax while another integrates these. Again, the particular needs of a given story must determine these matters.

The Beginning, Middle, and End pattern exists regardless of the surface organization of the action or mode of production. Greek tragedy alternated choral song and dance with enacted scenes in open amphitheatres, opera replaces dialogue with song and employs an orchestra in an orchestra pit to let music supply significance and underscore emotion. Medieval plays often performed different parts of the action on sequential wagons surrounded by festive mobs. Elizabethan drama used an open theater and an apron stage with minimal scenery to give verbally rich stories a cinematic flow of action. Our own screenplays are verbally terse, filmed actions projected on flat screens.

The means of an immediate, sequential, enacted, illusory imitation of action falling into a Beginning, Middle, and End within the larger fundamental story pattern is always the same, as is the end of all drama: to master experience, delight in illusion, permit escape from our daily concerns, and educate as we convey something of the truth that eludes us in reality.

14. Revelation, Clarity, Truth

Revelation and clarity are continuous in good writing, not just characteristics of the Climax and resolution.

The story of the slashed whore has grown in the telling when the Schofield Kid first appeals to Munny for his help in the Beginning of *Unforgiven*, a revelation with different meanings for us and Munny. Yet Munny refuses to help: he reveals he has been reformed by his late wife, and no longer drinks or kills.

Ada is amazed when Baines abruptly gives her the piano in the Middle of *The Piano*. He reveals he feels their "deal" is making her a whore and that what he really wants is her love.

Father Barry whispers that Johnny Friendly is betting Terry cannot get on his feet after the beating he suffers at the End of *On the Waterfront*. As we have seen, when Terry staggers up the ramp and leads the longshoremen to work on his own, he reveals he has what it takes to lead now.

Each stage of the development of the complications brings greater clarity with it too, although a character may also feel confused by additional complications, as is Book in *Witness* when he discovers the depth of the corruption facing him. Nikita in *La Femme Nikita* is devastated by her experience in Venice, but we see that she is caught in a lifestyle she won't be able to maintain.

The action, character, and conflict are clarified and revealed in response to the questions we continue to ask from the start, scene by scene: who is there, why, what stops them from doing what they want, what do they do about it, what's the point of it all? When we experience the final clarity and revelation achieved in the End, as well as see the simultaneous resolution of past and present problems, we experience the illusion that the truth has been revealed and established and a symbolic wholeness achieved that we feel momentarily as our own. We feel that we completely understand these characters and their story—just the kind of understanding that is almost always lacking in reality.

Art and truth are not opposed: screenwriting is the dramatic means by which we vicariously wrestle a shape and meaning for our experience through the struggles of the characters. The discovery of even imagined truth is deeply pleasurable; without that sense of truth films baffle and disappoint no matter how spectacular their effects.

III Dramatic Reality

1. Emotions Make Real

Our sense of reality is deeply plastic: we can believe in *Star Wars* equally with *Kramer vs. Kramer* or *The Virgin Spring.* But what makes these more than just images that follow consistent rules? What creates our sense of the *dramatic* reality of these stories? When we see Princess Leia's defenders in *Star Wars* show fear and anticipation of the impending attack, we begin to engage with the story: when the robots argue just like we might do over what direction to take on Tatooine, we engage more deeply: which way *is* the help they need? When R2-D2 is alone and realizes he is being watched and, perhaps, is in danger, the movements and sounds given what is a barely animated metal can convince us that it is a *character* experiencing the *appropriate emotion* for him to have—fear. That makes R2-D2 and his situation real to us.

Dramatic reality is experienced as emotional reality.

We must be able to engage with the characters emotionally; their emotions must be *appropriate* to their situation, or we can never engage with the story; its images remain devoid of emotional content and become boring. The story happens in us, or nothing happens at all (I, 5).

This is true for all styles, and what makes anything beyond obvious realism possible. Oedipus in *Oedipus Rex* first reassures the citizens that he is awaiting word from the oracle to understand the cause of the plague gripping Thebes, a reasonable course of action, then engages in a series of increasingly angry confrontations with his wife's brother, Creon, and the blind prophet, Teiresias. Oedipus is a proud man who won his throne through wisdom, not inheritance; when Teiresias first stonewalls, then accuses him of being the cause of the plague, Oedipus thinks he has been set up. Creon urged Teiresias on him. If Oedipus goes, Creon becomes king. Oedipus turns on Creon.

All his reactions, then, make elementary emotional sense. Far from seeing an actor in buskins and wearing a mask, we relate to a man because of the force and pertinence of his emotional response to his immediate circumstances. *That emotional sense simultaneously makes his dramatic circumstances feel real too.*

Julie becomes meaningful to us at the start of *Blue* entirely through her emotional reactions to the details of the accident that has killed her family. She is stunned, helpless, and when she is able to get out of bed, tries to commit suicide. That is sad but understandable; it makes her, and her world, real to us.

2. Identification, Empathy, Sympathy, and Fascination

> *Emotions make real; identity makes another's reality our own.*

Identification is a primal force on a par with our will to believe, and it appears as outright identification, empathy, sympathy, and fascination.

We identify with R2-D2 or Julie because the character's emotions let us put ourselves in his or her place. Identification is so central yet so commonplace in our experience of screenplays that we forget what a powerful and supple tool it is. Depth psychologists believe that our ability to project ourselves into the minds and feelings of others or to introject others into our own minds is an innate capacity: without it we could not relate to one another, let alone tell stories. Once we identify with a character, all the ensuing incidents then take on the same vivid emotional reality for us as for the character.

Sometimes in our dealing with characters, straightforward identification changes into *empathy*. Empathy need not involve liking. We don't identify with the corrupt Captain Schaefer in *Witness,* but when he turns in defeat from the Amish who meet him, Book, and Rachel as they leave the barn in the End, and sags to his knees, beaten, we feel his despair empathetically: his response is emotionally appropriate and evocative too. A character's appropriate emotional response gives a story's reality the same weight whether gained through empathy or identity.

Sympathy is another name that we give to this plastic force of identification. We feel sympathy for the characters we identify with, though less when we only empathize. It is basically our sense of approving fellow feeling.

Sheer force of personality and emotional appropriateness in even an evil character fascinate us and make that character and the reality he inhabits real to us. Villains exist as possibilities within ourselves; it is the forbidden that fascinates. Our minds are aroused and bound by even the most negative elements, dancing around them in fascination or the flip side, in revulsion. Experiencing a villain's demise, at its deepest level, lets us enjoy the illusion that we have been cleansed. Richard in *Richard III* is deceitful, untrustworthy, lying, audacious, intelligent, supremely manipulative, and gripping. We hate him and applaud his victories and ultimate death equally. We watch with horrified fascination as the Emperor and Darth Vader plot and gloat and almost win in the *Star Wars* trilogy. We cheer as the Emperor is destroyed, and we begin to like Darth Vader for his last-minute defense of his son, Luke, in *Return of the Jedi.*

Evil characters who are psychopaths cease to be characters. We may dread them through our identification with other characters, but as unreasoning forces of nature, as evil made manifest through psychic breakdown.

Identification can be turned to unexpected uses. We meet Will

Munny sympathetically at the start of *Unforgiven* as a struggling pig farmer and a father with two young children, a man trying to maintain a reformed character that he credits to his late wife. He is easy to identify with. But he coolly shoots the first cowboy, then in the Climax the unarmed brothel owner, Slim, and Little Bill and his deputies. When he threatens to kill anyone who shoots at him as he leaves, and their wives and children, he is believed—and we realize that this man we identified with is a killer of the first order. The implication, thanks to our identification, is that we are like him. That cuts uncomfortably close to the bone, but one look at our past century's history makes denial impossible.

Verbal is small, weak, and crippled in *The Usual Suspects*. Kujan is actually a good cop trying to sort out the truth about some violent criminals, but he comes across as a bully. We don't like him; we sympathize with Kujan but identify with Verbal. Yet "Verbal," we discover, is the devil incarnate. Through identification we are forced to realize that the devil can still take us in. We're not as smart or as good as we think.

A screenwriter can take us anywhere once our identification is made: it is a ring through our noses. Once made, the underlying psychic forces in which drama roots find a symbolic outlet through the mask of the character(s) that we wear in a story. Assuming their feelings have been appropriate and made the characters' realities convincing, then, through our identification with the characters, the implications of the story, whatever they are, become true for us, too.

3. Story, Dramatic, and Running Times

Our sense of identification is plastic, but so, too, is our sense of time: years, even eons, as in *2001*, can go by in the few hours actually needed to view a story. This is another commonplace that has profound implications. The time involved in a story's overall content is Story Time, referring to the fundamental story pattern; the time covered in its enacted portion is Dramatic Time; its actual performance time is Running Time.

The Great Lord Hidetora Ichimonji in *Ran*, Kurosawa's version of King Lear, has raised three sons and grown old. As the screenplay starts he apportions his power among his sons, imagining that he will remain the Great Lord anyway. In all that time he has been blinded by his own self-importance and failed to see their true natures. He banishes the youngest, Saburo, who truthfully tells him that his act is folly. By the end of the film Ichimonji and all his sons are dead or about to be killed. Running Time is roughly three hours, and Dramatic Time is several months, while Story Time includes their earlier life as well as the months evoked during Dramatic Time.

A screenwriter can use these disparities as a critical element in the action by manipulating our sense of cause and effect.

Hamlet meets his father's ghost in *Hamlet* and is commanded to seek revenge. In a cause-and-effect sequence he questions himself, deals with Rosencrantz and Guildenstern, Polonius, and Ophelia, then takes advantage of the arrival of the Players to plan a trap for Claudius's conscience. End of the Beginning. But we discover from other characters that actually months have passed without Hamlet's doing anything. This makes us aware of the illusory nature of the action in both Dramatic Time and in our experience of its cause-and-effect nature in Running Time. This is true of the play and all filmed versions. The same experience repeats in the ensuing Middle and End. On the one hand, we are made conscious of the illusory nature of the imitation of the action we are viewing, on the other, we feel as Hamlet does, that action is an illusion. Rather than destroying our belief, in this instance it gives our experience of the story a profound meaning.

Any dramatic element, however commonplace, can be turned to unexpected and original ends.

4. Cause and Effect: Immediacy and Meaning

A screenwriter must create an immediate cause-and-effect progression of the action through the reverses, scenes, sequences, complications, Beginning, Middle, and End. That progression maintains a story's dramatic reality and cohesion and creates an underlying expectation in the audience with the force of a syllogism that by the End all will inevitably climax and be made clear.

Schindler wines and dines the Nazi brass, gaining their friendship at the start of *Schindler's List,* because he wants to land army contracts and Jewish labor for his factory. Because Laura in *Beyond Rangoon* has her passport stolen, she must remain in Rangoon after her tour group leaves until the U.S. Embassy can issue her a new one. Because Terry forcefully makes Charley realize he is once again betraying him, Charley lets Terry leave the taxi in *On the Waterfront.* Ada accepts Baines's deal in *The Piano* because she wants her piano. Kane tosses his star in the dust in *High Noon* because he despises the townspeople who betrayed him in his hour of need.

All individual moments in the immediate cause-and-effect stream of action are transparent in good writing, meaning they are a specific action undertaken in response to a specific problem. Ada, Schindler, Hamlet, Oedipus, Book, Kane, Terry, Ted, or Charlie (in *Roxanne*) act in perfectly apparent, immediately cause-and-effect ways. Complexity in character and conflict does not arise from undefined actions, but from one individually clear action juxtaposed against the next.

This cause-and-effect stream of action is how a screenwriter answers and builds on those questions first posed at the Beginning and then carried through the screenplay: who is here, where is here, what are they doing, why are they doing that, what keeps them there, what do they do to solve their problem(s)? Causality links a story's incidents and makes sense of the characters and their actions.

This causal sequence and related sense of meaningfulness are not the same as the vision or idea that a screenplay may communicate, but only the means of that vision's communication, the manner in which the action works. Causality does, however, create an ultimate demand for a larger, explanatory meaning; when that is absent, we are frustrated (VI). A key reason that even escapist and lighthearted entertainments please despite the banality of their visions is that their real point is the cause-and-effect nature of the action itself, i.e., that behavior makes sense.

This illusion of causation can be turned to self-conscious uses just as the difference between Story, Dramatic, and Running Times is in Hamlet.

For example, Kurosawa's *Rashomon* retells the same encounter from the perspective of a bandit, a raped wife, a murdered husband (through a medium), and a frightened peasant. Each character's story is an equally credible cause-and-effect sequence of action that portrays the same action differently. That makes us aware of the illusory nature of Rashomon's storytelling. Kurosawa uses that awareness to make us feel that one man's truth is another's lie. We can never know causality, what act leads to what reaction; hence the truth is unknowable. Our inability to tell or realize what the truth is defines our humanity and points to a source of its depravity.

The Usual Suspects uses this device, too. At the End we realize that Verbal's story has mixed fantasy and truth in proportions that we will never be able to determine, and leaves us in much the same position as *Rashomon* does.

Yet both of these films show that even when we want to show the illusory nature of causation, dramatic action can do so only by showing cause-and-effect connections between immediate events and behavior. The attempt to communicate the illusory nature of causation by writing chaotically leads only to confusion.

Thus stories can make us aware that our innate senses of time and causation are illusory, confirming our worst fears.[19] But discovering the truth is one of our great pleasures, heightened in drama by being discovered through the instinctive pleasure of illusion (I, 2). Art redeems all that disquiets in reality through illusion, and by doing so, makes it bearable.

5. Necessary and Probable

Ideally, every element and every moment in a screenplay should be necessary and probable. Screenwriters are sometimes puzzled when told they have an interesting premise, a Beginning, Middle, and End structure, interesting characters, conflict, a cause-and-effect pattern to the incidents, an interesting vision or point, a crisis in their Crisis and a climax in their Climax—yet their screenplays have little merit. Why? Because too much is not probable, or, if probable, not necessary for the action.

Is it necessary and probable that Charley is sent to talk to Terry by Johnny Friendly in *On the Waterfront,* either to assure his silence before the criminal investigation that is starting up or to bring him to 437 River Street, where Johnny Friendly may have him killed? Yes: Charley is Johnny's right-hand man, Terry is Charley's responsibility, Terry knows too much to let him talk, and Charley as his brother is the most likely to succeed with him.

Once the two of them are together, everything Charley or Terry brings up is probable and necessary for the action: the bribe Charley offers for Terry's silence, Terry's conscience, and Charley's rage at the thought that Terry might act against his "friends." It is probable that Charley would pull a gun to emphasize the gravity of the situation, but not that he would use it, and he lets Terry push it aside. At a dead end, Terry makes a gesture that is natural for him, and it triggers a key memory of former betrayal. That too is likely, as is Charley's being moved to let Terry go because of Terry's reproach that Charley is still betraying him. Johnny Friendly has been established as a killer who will not let sentiment threaten his power, and since Charley fails him, he has Charley killed. Everything follows inevitably, probably, and necessarily.

The Professional opens as Leon artfully kills an entire gang of thugs and captures their leader. This establishes Leon's abilities, starts the story with a bang, defines its nature and style, captures our interest, and propels us forward. It is an adroit stylistic variation of the kind of opening that is typical for a crime action film, but it is all fantastic, and it is neither probable nor necessary to establish Leon as a good hit man.

Climactically, Leon is discovered by the corrupt, pursuing detective, Stan. A SWAT team is sent to get him, but Leon is so lethal that eventually it seems that a whole regiment armed with artillery is required to attack him. Even so, Leon survives a bomb explosion that wrecks the building and almost escapes, disguised as a wounded officer. Stan ambushes him, only to be blown up by Leon, along with himself. It is necessary that there be a final confrontation between Stan and Leon, but, for the rest, the action is wholly improbable, though colorful. We look for colorful sequences to top those in earlier films of the same genre (like action or science fiction films): such sequences are entertainments, elements of spectacle, and they easily slide into the comedic. But no one for a moment would compare the quality of *The Professional* to that of *On the Waterfront*. In fact, what gives *The Professional* its real interest is the story that develops between Matilda, a girl just entering puberty whose family Stan destroys, and Leon, who saves her and is spiritually rejuvenated as a consequence.

"Necessary and probable" in practice, then, is a standard that functions on several levels. It may apply to only part of the action, as in *The Professional* and genre writing generally; it may apply to the action but not to the premise, as in much science fiction; or it may apply to all aspects of a film. The greater a story's ambition to connect meaningfully with our deepest concerns, the more we will demand that all its elements be necessary and probable.

In *Beyond Rangoon* we are puzzled by Laura's dashing out at night into a dangerous situation involving a military confrontation; Tom's climactic narration in *Waterland* is entirely improbable in setting. A drama urging social action must convince us from Beginning to End, as in *Norma Rae,* or we will discount the film's message. In a tragedy, which cuts most deeply to the bone, as *The Virgin Spring,* or in drama of great ambition generally, as *The Godfather* or *Chinatown* or *High Noon* or *Casablanca* or *Gone with the Wind* or . . . we will demand that everything be necessary and probable: anything that is not will dilute the story's credibility and let us escape its perceptions.

6. Irrational Versus Improbable Elements

We are comfortable with terms like creativity, originality, and storytelling, but our prejudice for rationality leaves us with no favorable or even neutral word for the irrational. Yet creativity draws on more than the merely conscious, rational part of the ego. A screenwriter's ability to imagine what is necessary and probable for his or her story is a function of insight, and that is a matter of individual genius, irrational and unteachable. Our will to believe, the delight aroused by good stories, identification and the feelings evoked through that means, even the apparent cause-and-effect sequence of action, are all illusory or irrational.[20]

Moreover, the first perfect play has yet to be written after 2,400 years. Some element of weakness is always going to be found in our screenplays, while their irrational root in the storytelling, mythopoetic instinct can never be denied without stifling creativity in its cradle.

Some irrationalities of character and action are legitimate parts of screenplays, all of which to some extent examine irrational behavior. The Great Lord's folly in *Ran* is a case in point. How could Ichimonji not realize that once he starts to surrender power there can be no end until it is all gone? The best means of dealing with such an irrationality is to challenge it directly in the action, which Kurosawa has Saburo do, underscoring it, forcing us to focus on its outcome. When Ichimonji does see his error, the events he has unleashed have moved far beyond his initial folly and have shown men to be playthings of a fate they cannot understand.

A character can be morally hurtful and irrational, like Amon Goetz in *Schindler's List*, and be both right for the story and true because we also know the story actually happened. In short, men do irrational things because we are irrational beings, and these aspects of reality are as much food for drama as any other element.

Improbability in storytelling, however, is a separate matter. Just as with irrationality, the improbable cannot be kept out of stories, because sometimes the reality imitated contains improbable elements. Not everything works according to reason. Remember the old adage, Nothing is stranger than truth. But all too often an improbability is an avoidable fault.

Some improbabilities concern detail. Imagine a scene that shows the presence of contemporary Italian guards at the Vatican. Anyone can make a mistake of detail, but it should be caught in a succeeding draft: the Vatican guards wear traditional Swiss costumes. Commonly known details need to be respected. A screenwriter creating a medical sequence must research the action so that his details at least seem accurate. Tab Murphy of *The Last of the Dogmen* researched Cheyenne dog soldiers and the markings of their arrows, neither of which could be supplied by ignorance, although we would be unlikely to know one arrow from another. We may survive errors of detail in a story far more easily than larger improbabilities, yet a screenwriter should get the information he needs to imagine his story convincingly.

Some things simply shouldn't be seen. The stage version of *Much Ado About Nothing* does not show the false seduction of Hero, only reports it: Kenneth Branagh's film version shows it, and leaves us wondering how Claudio could be so easily deceived looking into a second-floor window twenty feet away.

Sophocles avoids a series of improbabilities by not showing Oedipus's lethal meeting with Laius at the crossroads in *Oedipus Rex,* or his marriage to Jocasta: why would even a rash young man in dread of killing his father kill someone old enough to be one? Or in dread of marrying his mother, marry a woman old enough to be her? How could a king be so poorly attended that Oedipus, alone, could overwhelm him?

These elements are part of the myth, and Oedipus believes his parents are safely at home in Corinth. Nonetheless, since these actions are not incorporated into the screenplay, their questionable nature is muted. There is an interesting psychic quirk at work here too: if the immediate action that we witness seems probable and necessary, we will attribute those qualities to improbable elements of action or backstory that are only reported. Immediate credulity can repair unseen or past improbability.

Some improbabilities are implicit in a premise, as for the *Star Wars* trilogy. But once the premise is granted, events are not improbable within it. We accept our ability to spin imaginary tales with imaginary elements that exist only within the reality of a given tale, so long as these elements are clearly established and work consistently (II, 5–6). Emotional reality is the crucial core of dramatic reality (see 1, above).

Stylistic or genre considerations may impel us toward improbabilities, as in the Beginning and Climax of *The Professional* (see 5, above). Such colorful entertainments are on a par with the dance routines in old Fred Astaire movies. What entertains at any given time is a function of popular fashion.

Nevertheless, the lack of an inner necessity for evil or irrational behavior remains a fault even in genre films. Stan's taking drugs and carrying out a bravura series of executions in *The Professional* doesn't sufficiently explain shooting a young girl in the back, a woman in a bathtub, or a little boy. When Stan stops, he is able to hold a rational conversation. The lack of plausibility makes it impossible for the sequence to convince even as an "entertainment." Stan is not a psychopath, and if he were, his being so would only function as an accepted shorthand for: I don't know his motivation; what does it matter, anyway? He's nuts. It's not very serious writing, unless we sense a genuine force of nature behind the characterization (see 2, above).

Dramatic considerations may lead us toward idealizations or emphases on aspects of reality that serve a story's vision, and not really be improbabilities. Norm, Paul, and their father in *A River Runs Through It* are larger-than-life figures: they are not given the intimate detailing, for example, of Jeff in *Rear Window*. We hardly notice that, though, because the style of the story highlights selected key moments, rather than accumulating all-but-the-kitchen-sink details.

The improbability of the portrayal of Book's world never arises in *Witness* because its violent or morally ambiguous scenes are appropriate to Book's milieu. The Amish and their values are weighed against those selected scenes and judged preferable. How would it have looked if Samuel had gone on a pleasant trip to the zoo? Are grimy bars and corrupt police all there is to Philadelphia?

Another way of putting these examples is this: both context and the governing vision of a story condition our sense of what is improbable.

However, a flawed premise that involves action that is improbable or inconsistent from any perspective is irremediable. Sloppy writing that contains obvious contradictions or uses coincidences in place of careful plotting is equally hopeless. A character consistently contradictory is a contradictory character; an unmotivated contradiction in a character or the action is sloppy storytelling.

We will insist, too, as we do with the standard of necessary and probable, that the more seriously we take a story, the less it make use of avoidable improbabilities or irrationalities.

Finally, beginning with Aristotle, critics have now and then held up a standard of "artistic correctness." Anything, let alone an improbability, contrary to artistic correctness is a problem. But usually when a critic applies such a standard he has a narrow version of drama in mind. Aristotle was concerned to defend the utility and elevation of tragedy. We know that drama fulfills deep needs through an immense variety of styles and stories and that utility is to be understood in a wider context than simply, as for Aristotle, purging the emotions of fear and pity. Sex and violence are frequently attacked, and their gratuitous use in drama is a fault just like any other. But drama, based on conflict, is inherently violent, whether emotionally or physically, while sex is as inevitable within drama as within our lives. All our greatest dramas involve violence, and most of them involve sexuality, from true love to rape and incest. Art exceeds its critics, as life its philosophers.

IV Storytelling Stance and Plot Types

1. The Action: Point of Attack and Its Context

A screenwriter wrestles with where to attack the story. Much of the fundamental story pattern must remain as backstory: where, then, should the action start? Moreover, a screenwriter must first face the task of establishing character and conflict before introducing the critical complication that generates the bulk of the action (II, 5–6, 11). That critical complication is our clue: *the point of attack is the complication that requires an unresolved problem from the past to appear progressively as a necessary element for the resolution of the protagonist's immediate problem.* That is the complication that incites the motion.

This is the murder witnessed by Samuel in *Witness*, the murder that Jeff suspects in *Rear Window*, the moment when Dave is asked to impersonate the president after his death in *Dave*; the moment in *Glory* when Shaw accepts command of a black regiment, the scene in which Don Vito denies his help to Sollozzo in *The Godfather*, and the point at which Ada's husband, Stewart, abandons her piano on the beach in *The Piano*. Kane decides to return to town to face the killers in *High Noon*, the president chooses to ask Sydney for a date in *The American President*; Julie fails to kill herself in *Blue*.

The complication that the point of attack introduces not only allows the past to enter the present; its omission would destroy the story. If Dave goes home after the president's death, that story never happens, nor does *Ran* if Ichimonji listens to Saburo and retains power. If Don Vito in *The Godfather* agrees to go into business with Sollozzo, Michael need never become involved.

Films like *Star Wars* or *Jurassic Park* only seem to start with the point of attack. Their action immediately slows to establish Luke and his conflicts and environs, and Alan, Ellie, and John. Establishing character and conflict creates a norm from which we can appreciate the problems generated by the point of attack. *The point of attack, in turn, guides us toward what needs to be established by way of context for it to be understood.* Failure to create a context, as in *Radioland Murders,* deeply disorients. *Witness* establishes Rachel, Samuel, and the Amish; *Roxanne* sets up the inept firemen, Roxanne's beauty, and Charlie's nose, intelligence, and superlative ability; *Ran* takes us through a hunt and a dream before Ichimonji declares his intention to surrender power.

When the key complication arrives within the context of this established "norm," the protagonists are launched on the road to realizing that they have lived an illusion. As that sinks in, they start to set their lives right so that they can once again return to a norm, now meaning a life truly free of illusion and conflict. That is always their central goal and, of course, the greater illusion with which a film leaves us.

2. Plot Complexity, Types, Variation, and Magnitude

Renaissance critics misread Aristotle and developed a theory of the "unities" of action, time, and place based on his *Poetics,* which held that a dramatic story should have a single action without subplots whose Dramatic Time should coincide with its actual Running Time, the dramatic story using only those locations possible to use in that Running Time.[21] The French classic drama of Corneille and Racine epitomizes this practice, but nothing could be farther from contemporary practice.

A screenplay today has an extended time frame, a main plot, and typically multiple subplots and settings like Shakespeare's plays. Our plotting tends to differ only in degree of complexity, not in kind. Films as simple as *Tender Mercies* or *Cross Creek* use subplots. A classically tight film like *High Noon* has subplots concerning Harvey and Kane's former mistress, and covers a Dramatic Time of an entire morning in a Running Time of an hour and a half. *Rear Window* observes unity of place but has many subplots concerning the people who are visible in other apartments; its Dramatic Time stretches over days, as does that of *Casablanca,* which has several subplots. *The Godfather* begins with a subplot to get Johnny a role in Hollywood, then weaves several more into action that covers years.

This multiply-threaded structure of our screenplays echoes our sense that reality is woven from many strands. That drama should echo reality in this respect is a prejudice that we learned from the theatrical reform at the end of the nineteenth century (I, 3). That drama should be multiply threaded is also an inheritance from medieval theater and, for us, from Elizabethan theater.

Our plots divide broadly into organic and episodic. *Kramer vs. Kramer* and *Tootsie* and *Blue* and *Fanny and Alexander* and *Casablanca* have organic plots in which one action develops inevitably and directly from the previous action; removal of any component would confuse the story. Episodic plots confront us with unrelated or barely related sequential adventures. Episodic plots, as in the various Indiana Jones films, compromise the standard of necessary and probable, while organic plots try to observe it.

Indiana Jones goes to Tibet to get a necessary artifact in *Raiders of the Lost Ark,* an artifact that Marion could just as well have held in New York or Shanghai, or on campus in a related but hostile department. It is probable that Jones finds the Ark in Egypt, but his carrying out his own dig in the midst of a larger, German one is amusing nonsense. His exploits to regain the stolen Ark have an air of "What can I do to top myself next?" rather than a sense of inevitability, as is expressed by Kane's actions in *High Noon*. No probability is involved when Jones rides across the Mediterranean on the deck of a submerged sub, although it is necessary that he follow the Ark.

Organic plots are the avenue to substantial comedic or dramatic writing. Actions at once inevitable and unexpected can be built up in such plots, like the steps that bring Michael to kill McCluskey and Sollozzo in *The Godfather*, or motivate Olivier in *Blue* to try to get under Julie's skin, or lead to the final revelation and Reverse in *The Usual Suspects*, or drive Ted into impersonating a woman in *Tootsie*.

This lack of organic structure does not detract from the imaginativeness of successful episodic films like *Raiders of the Lost Ark* or diminish their success as colorful entertainments; we just don't look to such stories for meaningful insight into human character or fate.

Many films repeat a Beginning or Middle structure. A Beginning 1 leads into a Beginning 2 in *A River Runs Through It*, as in *2001*. In *Lawrence of Arabia* a Middle 1 leads into a Middle 2. Ends are not duplicated. The turning point at the end of a Beginning 1, like Norman's return from college in *A River Runs Through It*, sets the terms of the next Beginning, when Norman faces the critical summer that will change all of their lives as he decides what to do with himself. Lawrence wins Feisal's support and heroically captures Aqaba, transforming the Arab revolt in the Middle 1 of *Lawrence of Arabia*, but he is also both reproached for the lack of hard money at Aqaba's fall and tastes despair and failure when he rashly crosses the Sinai and one of his young servants dies. In the Middle 2 he torments the Turks with guerrilla warfare until in the pause caused by winter he rashly dares fate by going to Deraa, where he is raped and beaten. Each Crisis threatens Lawrence's ability to lead, and each must be overcome.

Each repeated Beginning or Middle repeats its structure, ending in a Crisis (if a Middle) or in a defining turning point (if a Beginning). Usually we repeat the Middle, although we always know that there is an underlying sense of beginning-middle-end that these repetitions allow us to dramatize effectively.

Even our most realistic and intimate stories have a larger-than-life magnitude because of the physical nature of viewing a film (I, 5). Serious thematic concern increases our sense of magnitude: *The Godfather* is a larger, more important film than *Sleepless in Seattle*, enjoyable as the latter may be. Costa-Gavras's *Z* has a political weight absent from *Kramer vs. Kramer*. *Smiles of a Summer Night* lacks the thematic sweep of *Chinatown* or *Dr. Zhivago*. Rating movies is an academic game; what matters here is recognition of a screenplay's ambition.

Magnitude may refer to length, too, though any movie whose immediate action doesn't support its Running Time will feel too long, as does *Orlando*, with its stately pacing. Some stories are naturally epic in length: *Gone with the Wind, Dr. Zhivago*, any of the *Godfather* trilogy, *Gandhi, Ran, Cleopatra, Fanny and Alexander, Lawrence of Arabia, Spartacus*, and many of the old Hollywood Roman or biblical epics. We don't object if the action requires and supports extended treatment and has appropriate thematic weight. However, four hours Running Time appears to be too much for memory or attention. Length married to thematic ambition and compelling action may equal a "big" film, but there is no shortage of important shorter films.

Finally, to avoid the confusion that attends various levels of beginning/middle/end, we will use the traditional terms Act 1 to mean the Beginning (II, 11), Act 2 for the Middle (II, 12), and Act 3 for the End (II, 13) in the discussion that follows. This traditional terminology avoids jargon and lets us refer without confusion to the three major parts of any screenplay, teleplay, or stage play regardless of the fact that screenplays are written without act breaks, teleplays may have as many acts as there are commercial breaks, and many stage plays have only one or two formal acts, or just a sequence of numbered scenes. The Beginning, Middle, and End structure referred to by Act 1, Act 2, and Act 3 is present in all these.

3. Dramatic Unity: Relating Subplots and Parallel Plots

A screenwriter struggles to relate various subplots to the plot or, in special cases, plots of equal standing within a given film so that the action is perceived as a progressive whole. Linking the heroine and hero is a typical plotting problem in Act 1 (II, 11). Dramatic unity is maintained by making sure that all the action bears necessarily and progressively on the protagonist's fate.

Subplots have their own beginning, middle, and end, however attenuated, and can relate to the main plot and characters in four overlapping ways. They can help establish the setting; they can have a cause-and-effect impact on the fortunes of the hero and the heroine; they can illuminate the hero or heroine, or the audience concerning them; and they can complement a particular stage in the main plot. Some, suitably brief, may function as comic relief, ironic comment, or satire.

Subplots that function in none of these ways are superfluous and disruptive.

Several of the subplots in *Rear Window* give substance to the setting that Jeff is reduced to watching. Others complement and illumine Lisa's situation ironically, as when her attempt to serve a "perfect" dinner backfires while we see Miss Lonely Hearts having dinner with an imaginary companion and Miss Torso dealing with wolves, both fates that Lisa is trying to avoid. Miss Lonely Hearts' prospective suicide affects Lisa's fortunes as Jeff calls the police before he needs them to save Lisa, which allows the police to save Lisa's life at the right moment. The couple whose dog is murdered in the Crisis influence Lisa and Jeff to go on pursuing the murderer. The Newlyweds are comic relief.

Book's discovery of Carter's murder in *Witness* provokes the violent action that gives him away. Harvey's lack of principle throws Kane's principled motivation into a sharp light in *High Noon;* his dismissal as a boy by Kane's former mistress underscores Kane's manliness. The opening subplot in *The Godfather* concerning Johnny's gaining a Hollywood role shows Don Vito's ruthlessness.

Split or parallel major plots are a different matter. Usually a screenplay has a predominant story line that subplots are easily related to, but sometimes plot lines of equal weight need to be related. These need to complement, illumine, or affect the other's plot and characters also, even in the rare cases when each plot could stand alone, as in *The Godfather II.*

In a superb display of dramatic irony, that film plays Don Vito's rise off against Michael's descent into the life that he and his father hoped he could avoid (VII, 5). That ironic contrast is driven home in Act 3 as Don Vito's triumphant, vengeful trip to Sicily with the young Michael in his arms contrasts with the murder of Fredo and Michael's memory of the day that he told his family he had joined the Marines, defying the family's moral stance and, in effect, declaring his independence. *Sleepless in Seattle* is less extreme, structurally. Although the protagonists pursue separate stories, they almost link a number of times while nearly succumbing to the wrong partners, finally joining at the end.

Separate or parallel plots are neither better nor worse than others, though they are less usual. Their success or failure is a function of a given story's needs, not of principle. Typically their Beginnings, Middles, and Ends unfold at the same time in Running Time. Major plot lines that aren't complementary and don't affect or illumine one another indicate badly organized screenplays.

4. Typical Story Patterns

We live in one of the great dramatic eras, the first in which screenwriting exceeds playwrighting in excellence, characterized by a breadth of storytelling rarely matched in the past. The contemporary screenwriter is constrained only by the need to hold a large, public audience, which keeps him focused on speaking to our broad and immediate concerns. He is the heir to a century that has opened our eyes to our range of angelic and bestial capacities and prepared us, as audience, to go on any journey that explores our heart but does not wholly outrage our sense of rightness, as difficult to define as that is. A fine screenwriter enjoys a stature sometimes superior to that of historians and psychologists, sociologists or philosophers, who are bound to facts, statistics, or limited systems. The dramatic story is a particular that stands for the universal, an act of the imagination that creates a set of characters whose fate, as we identify or empathize with them, speaks to all of us, illuminating our lives with bright light or long, complex shadows.

These stories tend to fall into recognizable and often overlapping patterns.

Tragedy, the story of a basically good man or woman moving to misfortune through his or her flaws, remains the most difficult of dramatic stories to write because of the unrelenting application of the standard of necessary and probable to its action. A story written so exactingly forces us to our deepest insights. *Nixon* follows such a pattern, though Nixon remains as unlikable a figure in the film as in life, as do *A Streetcar Named Desire* and *The Virgin Spring*.

The pattern of rewarding the good and punishing the bad is as popular with us as with audiences in Aristotle's time. Such dramas are tragicomedies where real pain may be inflicted and suffered, yet the final outcome is happy, which led Aristotle to classify them as comedies. They reflect the common hope of men and women at all times that justice and love will prevail, a hope easily abused in fact and, in film, through superficial writing.

A character overcoming his or her flaws is a related popular pattern, such as Ted becoming a good father in *Kramer vs. Kramer,* or Kane mastering his fear in *High Noon.*

But we are fascinated with evil too, and we enjoy bad men rising, thriving, and finally being punished in films like *Scarface, Richard III,* or *Little Caesar.* The endings of such stories, which usually confirm our moral stance, reassure our guilty pleasures.

Redemption stories appeal to our sense of lost innocence, combined with the hope that desire and effort can give us a second chance. Typically, a good man falls or has fallen, then rises again when given a climactic second chance. Darth Vader spends three films doing evil, yet in the end destroys the Emperor in *Return of the Jedi.* Terry is transformed from a bum to a leader in *On the Waterfront.* A singer is reborn through love in *Tender Mercies.* The prodigal son who comes home is a theme as old as the Bible, while multiple Samson and Delilah films have the fallen Samson redeeming himself at the end.

The corruption of good men or women dismays us as they fall from integrity, but it is at the heart of some of our best stories. Michael, in *The Godfather* trilogy, is a tragic figure, a good man whose success is a failure as he turns evil through circumstance and love for his father (or, in Aristotelian terms, pity). Munny is a reformed killer in *Unforgiven;* we accept his return to killing as justified vengeance. The heroine in *Rashomon* is raped, but after that we can't tell whether she assented, refused, wished her husband to be killed, or killed him herself. Charles Van Doren destroys his golden boy image despite confessing in *Quiz Show.*

Innocent and good characters who fail make us uncomfortable but populate our stories also, like the innocent Tom in *To Kill a Mockingbird,* or Luke in *Cool Hand Luke,* whose punishment far exceeds his crime. The former's fate is part of that film's attack on bigotry, while Luke is intended to convey indomitability. Brubaker fails in *Brubaker,* for he is too idealistic a warden for the prison (read: real) world, though one particular mess is cleaned up.

We even tolerate evil men moving from frustration to success. The cannibal Hannibal Lecter in *The Silence of the Lambs* helps the heroine and promises to leave her alone when he escapes, in the end marking a hypocrite for his next meal. Verbal's true nature in *The Usual Suspects* is hidden until the end, when he gets away. Yet the pure success of a bad character with no redeeming qualities rubs us the wrong way. That the world rewards success, not morality, offends our sense of rightness, which is a morally proper stance, if unrealistic.

Many of our best screenplays and plays are family stories. These may fall within any pattern. The *Godfather* trilogy is a family story, as are *Kramer vs. Kramer* and *Hamlet* and *Oedipus Rex* and the *Star Wars* trilogy and *Ran.* The consequences of action for other family members are immediately apparent; their closeness allows a screenwriter to build conflicts of depth more easily.

Science fiction and fantasy, while genres themselves, exemplify underlying patterns of the heroic redemption of civil society and the achievement of mental cohesion as old as the mythic hero and "hero-as-ego-archetype" patterns (I, 2). The protagonist(s) overcome monsters to establish civic society and/or the possibility of rational behavior, whether the monster is a titan in *Clash of the Titans,* Martian invaders in *War of the Worlds,* the Emperor in the *Star Wars* trilogy, or the body-snatching Ra of *Stargate. Godzilla* came from a Japan traumatized by loss and upheaval.

Genres are congealed story treatments with conventional expectations that may fall into many patterns. We expect high-tech marvels in sci-fi, an ambivalent view of character and reality in film noir, zany behavior in slapstick comedy, pistols, Stetsons, and horses in westerns. We expect a revisionist western to show a film noirish slant of character and outcome. In fantasy we expect the supernatural to be blended with medieval technologies, wizards, talking dragons or even stranger beasts, and conflict-resolving quests. Action films are often episodic, and they must have ever more breathtaking sequences of action, particularly of chase scenes, those quintessential entertainments that we currently demand.

These conventional expectations let a screenwriter and audience assume broad characteristics of a story's reality in advance, allowing audiences to judge variations and execution in reference to other films. But such "conventionalization" also substitutes entertainment fads for dramatic writing, as in the action sequences of the *Lethal Weapon* series or *The Professional* (III, 5).

Finally, certain elemental patterns emerge naturally in intense good writing that are not deliberately intended by a screenwriter. *Beowulf* shows an archetypal pattern of the youthfully awkward hero who achieves respect and fame through destroying a monster. *On the Waterfront* falls into this archetypal pattern as well when Terry moves from being a bum to being the leader of the longshoremen as he overcomes Johnny Friendly. The western variant with a "dude" as hero shows a similar pattern. Writing archetypally deliberately and avoiding pretentiousness is hard, although Joseph Campbell's involvement with George Lucas on the *Star Wars* trilogy is an exception. More often, writing falls into such archetypal patterns naturally because our fundamental experience does so (I, 2; V, 1).

5. Narration, Flashback, Fragmented Action

Narration is a device that new writers, especially, should resist. When it is effective, narration provides an *additional* plot element. It should not substitute for action or tell us what is already apparent.

Narration is a typical device in detective stories, like Marlowe's reflections in *The Big Sleep*, which show Marlowe's drive toward knowledge or give colorful evaluations without substituting for action. Old Norm makes it clear in *A River Runs Through It* that he is telling the story at his father's urging in order to find its truth. His narrative only frames a perspective, placing our focus on his goal of truth-finding. *Star Wars* and *The Last of the Mohicans* both open with narrative titles to set unusual conditions.

In contrast, Laura's moments of narration in *Beyond Rangoon* are unnecessary; there is nothing in them that is not communicated better by the action. The narration in *The Last of the Dogmen* actually substitutes for action and states the obvious.

Flashback speaks to the fluidity of our sense of time and accords with how we feel our minds work, constantly mixing memory and immediate concerns. We simply do not exist very much in the present, and neither should our characters and stories if we want to evoke a convincing symbolic sense of reality. Flashback is endemic in *Citizen Kane, Waterland, Suddenly Last Summer, Cries and Whispers, The Godfather II,* and *The Usual Suspects.* But many effective films make no use of it—consider *The Big Sleep* and *Schindler's List.*

A flashback must be immediately motivated in the cause-and-effect flow of the action, and all flashbacks must help define the immediate action or move it forward. Michael in *The Godfather II* remembers joining the Marines when he hoped for a life apart from the family after he has his brother Fredo killed. The flashbacks in *The Usual Suspects* are driven by Verbal's need to respond to Kujan. *Waterland* expands the flashback device into a class trip into Tom's past, undertaken immediately to prove that history makes sense to his class and to understand how he and his wife have reached their present crisis. An unmotivated flashback, or one that explains nothing, is ineffective and a fault.

Finally, sometimes a screenplay's scenes are fragmented: we encounter a scene's beginning here, its middle there, its end elsewhere, mingled with fragments from other scenes and symbolic snippets of action. Sometimes when one part of a scene clearly predicts another, that section is rightly left to the imagination. A woman's resistance melts in a man's arms, or a killer bares his knife; next we find ourselves in the morning after, or at a funeral.

But these scene fragments can be assembled in sequences and turned into a screenwriting technique. Sometimes such sequences are fragmented as well and mixed with others, as happens in *Citizen Kane* because of intervening flashbacks. The impact of such writing is at once swift, immediate, distancing, and potentially confusing as a general technique. It is not used substantially in most screenplays. There are notable exceptions, like *Citizen Kane,* and Godard's *Breathless* in 1959; imitators of the latter soon ran out of steam. The technique tends to put the audience in the role of a mosaic artist, assembling a story's sense piece by piece. Montage uses this technique, as we see at the start of Cocteau's *The Blood of a Poet* (I, 4).

Such quintessentially cinematic screenwriting paradoxically demands the kind of strenuous imaginative participation characteristic of Elizabethan dramaturgy.

6. Exceptions

There is hardly any screenwriting "rule" that someone cannot find an exception for, while there are as many structural variations as there are screenplays. A screenwriter who forgets this is in danger of becoming repetitive and obvious.

Although all screenplays do have Acts 1, 2, and 3, the key structural elements in *Four Weddings and a Funeral* are each wedding and the funeral generated by the death in the third wedding. The fourth wedding corresponds entirely to Act 3, or the End, but the Act 1 turning point falls in the middle of the second wedding. This is not experienced as a disparity or a problem.

Keaton's helpless reinvolvement in subsequent crimes in *The Usual Suspects* is the turning point at the end of Act 1, and the gang's inability to avoid Keyser Soze's order to attack the ship is the Crisis. But it is the paired interactions between Kujan and Verbal after the establishing character and conflict phase that drive the action: each challenge by Kujan leads Verbal into a more revealing flashback and provides the real sense of the story's movement.

The fate of the main character is usually co-extensive with the story, but Karin is killed in the Crisis of *The Virgin Spring*. Normally this kind of event would disrupt continuity and identification, but we avoid that disruption and a sense of anticlimax as Karin's father becomes the protagonist in Act 3 because the story is not done, he was prepared for in Act 1, and we want Karin's killers punished. Mariko's death in *Shogun* does lead in a more predictable way to a sense of anticlimax in the concluding action.

A screenwriter writes actions emphasizing behavior more than other dramatists do (I, 4), yet certain films are inactive, or would be devastated if the emphasis were removed from their dialogue (VII, 3). *My Dinner with Andre* is a good film, limited in setting and appeal, consisting of charged, emotional dialogue, as if it were a stage play; the same is true of a significant part of *Frankie and Johnny*. *Lolita*'s impact depends on sometimes witty, sometimes pretentious literary dialogue.

Finally, as touched on in 4, above, the dramatic structure of a genre film can be reduced to a skeleton fleshed with entertainments made up of spectacle, special effects, or action sequences justified only in reference to previous, similar films.

V Character

1. Sources and Types

What do we mean by *character*? Characters are *imagined men and women of any age drawn from the heart,* people like Ada and Baines of *The Piano,* or Hamlet, or Book and Rachel of *Witness,* or Ted and Joanna of *Kramer vs. Kramer,* even people that are creatures with human attributes like the centipede or glowworm in *James and the Giant Peach,* or mechanisms like the robots in *Star Wars.* The centipede in *James and the Giant Peach* who hungrily imagines that a seagull has become a flying cooked carcass is different only in appearance from the Little Tramp's hungry companion in *The Gold Rush* who sees him as a chicken to be plucked and cooked.

A character, like a conflict, can be drawn from newspapers or dreams, personal experience or a friend; he or she can be discovered in history or myth, the media or the imagination, or be based on a stranger encountered in a chance meeting. Almost anything can spark the creation of a character.

A screenwriter may find a character talking to him in a twilight state and be *compelled* to find his story. Or a story may demand the development of a particular character, whom a screenwriter laboriously constructs, for either a plot or a character can be primary in a screenplay. Deciding which element is primary on principle is like asking whether the chicken or the egg comes first. Characters saddled with poor plots inhabit weak screenplays, as do good plots bound to poorly drawn characters.

Character, as well as situation and conflict, becomes real to us through emotion (III, 1). A character must touch our hearts. If Richard in *Richard III* or Verbal in *The Usual Suspects* fails to touch our hearts, if the robots and insects of *Star Wars* and *James and the Giant Peach* remain just mechanisms and insects, they don't come alive as characters and cannot arouse emotion, and without emotion there can be no effective screenplay. The essence of the various forms of identification is that the characters are the masks we wear, images of ourselves when we look into the mirror of the action. Even psychopaths and monsters like the creature in *Alien* come from somewhere in our imagination and hearts.

Once a character captures a screenwriter's attention, it means that character has lodged within his mind beyond the cognitive level and now gives a face to some conflict or drive that a screenwriter distances himself from by putting it into a screenplay. A successful character takes root in the same inchoate depths in each member of the audience.

Some characters hit a popular chord and are exploited in sequels, like Rocky in *Rocky*. Sometimes a character holds a genuine obsession for a dramatist. Sophocles returned to Oedipus at the end of his career; Shakespeare populated several plays with Falstaff, then killed him off in *Henry V* to get him out of the way. Falstaff has reached independent life in opera in Verdi's *Falstaff*. Michael in all three and Don Vito in the first two of *The Godfather* films are characters of obsessive interest. Spock in the *Star Trek* series has proved to be a character of compelling interest with his very human struggle between logic and passion: two of the *Star Trek* films deal with his death and resurrection.

Certain character types are as old as Menander's New Comedy in classic Greece and the Roman Comedy of Plautus and Terence: the young lover, the ingenue, the compromised woman (courtesan), the braggart (typically a soldier), the busybody or meddler in one form or another. We have added many new figures, like the demanding ethnic mother-in-law, the rebellious son, the unsuitable boyfriend brought home by the daughter, the bearded revolutionary, the more or less incompetent psychiatrist, the lantern-jawed, laconic cowboy. These are resources to draw on and vary, sometimes even to develop into strong characters, like the Nurse in *Romeo and Juliet* or Emma in *Emma*. These types endure because they are based on common aspects of personality and behavior.

We are unable to shake our fascination with the archetypal hero, even in the traditional form of Hercules, or in modern versions, like Clark Kent in *Superman*. Book in *Witness* and Kane in *High Noon* are heroes, as are Munny in *Unforgiven* or Indiana Jones in *Raiders of the Lost Ark*, or Dave in *Dave*.

Some characters are so deeply imagined, and the story they inhabit so intensely felt, that they unexpectedly fall into archetypal patterns, like Terry in *On the Waterfront* (I, 2; IV, 4). Nikita embodies the Pygmalion myth in *La Femme Nikita* as she is reshaped from an addict and killer into a woman who finally cannot bear violence. Shaw's *Pygmalion* and its Lerner and Lowe musical and film version, *My Fair Lady*, give more traditional Pygmalion variants. Beauty and the Beast stories provide a pattern as a manbeast is saved by a woman, whose love symbolically tames the man and her own fear of sexuality, as in Cocteau's *Beauty and the Beast*.

A screenwriter may be unaware that a character falls into one of these patterns until late in working on a story with its usual contemporary subject and setting, if awareness dawns at all. A character who falls into such a pattern naturally has a tremendous impact, expressing something basic to our common fantasy and experience.

This is a key to the grip that characters can have on us and the special force of drama. As characters struggle to make sense of their experience, we, through the power of identification, feel ourselves making sense of experience, the thing that is so elusive in reality, and at times doing so with such intensity that we live on an archetypal level of common humanity (I, 2; III, 2). To do so fills us with elation.

2. Force, Consistency, Change, Truth

We find ourselves caught up by characters as diverse as Jesus in *The Last Temptation of Christ* and Hannibal Lecter in *The Silence of the Lambs,* the psychopath in *Seven,* or Verbal in *The Usual Suspects,* as we have seen. Our basic requirement for belief in a character is not goodness but force of characterization: a character who repels but fascinates can hold us as well as one we like and with whom we overtly identify.

Force of characterization, however, applies to all characters. Weakly characterized personages are just that—weak. Even minor characters are forcefully characterized in good writing, like the secondary characters in *Rear Window* who on occasion prove so essential to the main action, or many of the supporting characters in *Ran.* The unseen newlywed wife in *Rear Window* is sharply characterized by her complaints at the end. Every character should stand out sharply in our mind's eye.

All characters need to be consistent. Whether a character is drawn directly from life or from the imagination, like Beetlejuice in *Beetlejuice* or the alien in *Alien,* he must remain consistent, or true to type, however that type is defined in a particular story. A braggart doesn't suddenly become modest. A resourceful character doesn't suddenly give up. James Bond can't reach some difficult obstacle, sigh, and throw in the towel. A character can't be a wallflower one moment and the belle of the ball the next. Gandhi doesn't become a killer, and no killer becomes Gandhi. Rachel in *Witness* doesn't act like a prostitute one moment and a nun the next, while a man blinded by ego and power like Ichimonji in *Ran* doesn't suddenly become a fount of wisdom.

This does not mean that a character may not feel a momentary inconsistency, such as doubt (Kane in *High Noon*), fear (Book in *Witness*), or savage fury (Romeo in *Romeo and Juliet* as he kills Tybalt).

Yet most of our characters, no matter how far they may find themselves from realistic situations, are consistent with or true to life emotionally, behaving in a manner that is appropriate to their given circumstances and more or less necessary and probable the more seriously we are expected to take them.

Yet the characters who mean the most to us are those who grow through the action. Change is as continuous for characters as for the dramatic obstacle in effective writing (II, 10). Even Hamlet grows, albeit in his own peculiar way, deepening as we watch him, his inaction used to reveal his motivation in an ever more deeply shadowed light. Blanche's failed effort to change moves us deeply and seals her fate in *A Streetcar Named Desire*.

Such change must be motivated through the action, step by step. Ted, in *Kramer vs. Kramer,* earns his change from an insensitive father to a great one and a better man by going through a developmental process that convinces us at each step of the way. Even then, he remains Ted; he isn't suddenly a baseball hero, or James Bond. Baines in *The Piano* changes by falling in love with Ada and releases her from their deal, winning her love in the process. Michael changes into his opposite through the action of *The Godfather.* The Hindu fanatic who killed a Muslim mother and child in retribution for the murder of his own son doesn't cease to be a tragic, driven man in *Gandhi.* He is contrite but understandably hopeless. We believe his change when Gandhi offers him a way out: to find an orphaned Muslim boy the same age as his dead son, and raise him as his own and as a Muslim, in penance.

These changes are revelations to us; they surprise and move us, cumulatively baring the heart and nature of characters, leading us to feel that we truly understood these people. Change leads inexorably toward that deeply pleasurable sense of discovering the truth. A scene or sequence without growth, without change, is dramatically dead and thwarts that deep pleasure.

3. Defining Character

Characters must be defined within the broad categories of consistency, change, being true to type and life, and force of characterization. Each detail of definition enriches the screenplay and fires a screenwriter's imagination, whereas the undefined is diffuse, and stultifies.

Each individual has an inner and outer life, past, personality, age, gender, race, physical appearance, style of dress, occupation, economic and social status, manner of speaking, and physical or behavioral traits. He may show representative acts, or possess a defining flaw. An inner life contains specific dreams and goals, fantasies, a character's real-world view, and irrationalities. These are at the heart of any character's behavior. A disturbed character is disturbed in some particular way; a dream or goal is always some particular dream or goal that drives a character forward and may or may not be supported by the character's outward life.

The outer life divides into a private aspect for friends and family and a public aspect for classmates, associates at work, or the world in general.

The past of major characters is crucial, and is developed in the backstory. It usually contains an unresolved event or problem, which may also be unrealized (I, 1; II, 11; IV, 1).

Each character has a particular personality, introverted or extroverted, hardheaded, a soft touch, or . . .

Each is gender-defined unless it is some special creation, as in *Star Wars* or *James and the Giant Peach*.

Although each belongs to a particular race or has a national or ethnic root, these are not always central.

Each has a particular physical appearance and a characteristic way of dressing. Imagine a fat, sweating man in a T-shirt, another thin, short man in a three-piece suit carrying an attaché case and wearing thick glasses, or another with the muscles of a body builder: each is suggestive in particular ways, while a character who is merely described as "average" is a cipher. A beautiful woman is beautiful in a particular way: a trashily dressed beauty suggests one line of development, a lovely woman in a classic Chanel suit suggests another.

Each character works or is supported in some specific way, whether as a drug dealer or a university president, a student, a wife, a concubine, or a labor agitator, like Norma in *Norma Rae*.

Each has a particular social and economic status. One is a Southern belle fallen on hard times, like Blanche in *A Streetcar Named Desire;* another is an uneducated proletarian, like Stanley Kowalski or his unimaginative friend Mitch. The characters may be middle-class Anglos, like Ted and Joanna in *Kramer vs. Kramer.*

Each has his or her own way of speaking. Some, like Blanche, have a poetry about them; others, like Kujan in *The Usual Suspect,* are full of declarative certainty. The variety is infinite, but always specific to each character.

Many have particular physical or behavioral traits that are part of their personality. Jeff in *Rear Window* has a leg in a cast, and, at the end, two; Charlie in *Roxanne* has a long nose; Josey Wales in *The Outlaw Josey Wales* spits before going into action; Nikita, in *La Femme Nikita,* can't smile at first. Rachel in *Witness* lacks coquetry.

Some have representative acts that typify or reveal key elements. Julie in *Blue* keeps her daughter's blue hanging beads, unable to break completely with the past; Nora in *A Doll's House* reveals a hidden defiance by sneaking macaroons. Terry falls back on a boxer's gesture in his confrontation with his brother in *On the Waterfront* and plays with a longshoreman's hook before going down to the docks to get his rights. Blanche wears red at a key moment in *A Streetcar Named Desire* and is haunted by a waltz. The hero exchanges a clerical collar for a gun in *Pale Rider.*

The many types on which a character may be based are reviewed in I, 2; III, 2; and IV, 4. Each is the cornerstone of a more complete characterization.

Often a character has a key flaw, like Book's violence in *Witness,* Sonny's hot temper in *The Godfather,* or Hamlet's indecision. This is not essential, however, even for tragic heroes. Michael in *The Godfather* is corrupted from love and fear for his father; Mrs. Mulwray in *Chinatown* is more sinned against than sinning; though Fenton tries in *Remains of the Day,* Stevens suffers the loss of love through an inability to reach out for it when he could; the pride and decisiveness of Oedipus bring about both his rise and his fall: are these characteristics flaws or virtues?

More broadly, flaws are present in most characters because we are all flawed, and the characters who reflect us, true to life as reviewed in section 2 above, are flawed too. We are not masters of reality, except for brief, transcendent moments. Our limitations define ourselves equally with our capacities. Ideal characters are inhuman and inherently boring.

4. Building and Revealing

We build and reveal characters through their enactment of the incidents of the plot in a cause-and-effect, minor reverse-by-reverse, scene-by-scene manner, guided by the governing vision of the screenwriter by which he or she selects and marshals the incidents for the chosen end (VI, 3). The result is powerful if the action also has a high degree of probability and necessity.

A screenwriter establishes character, conflict, and dramatic reality through a character's emotions and ensuing actions in response to the initial problem(s). A screenwriter builds a character as the sequential, immediate, conflicted situations in which the character is placed bring out fresh aspects of personality and capacity as he or she tries to cope with each new and unanticipated shape of the dramatic obstacle (II, 10, 13–14). Growth is a cumulative, revelatory process.

Moreover, we must see a character be passionate if we are to believe him or her capable of passion; or full of violence if able to kill, if we are to understand that as part of his or her makeup. All that we can experience in a screenplay is what we see or hear. By the end of Act 3 we should feel we have lived a character through and through.

A character's immediate goal is always to solve his immediate problem; the ultimate goal is always to reach the end of conflict on his or her terms, or happiness. A character's vision of what such happiness means may change.

At the beginning of *The Godfather,* Michael is a young, handsome, decorated soldier; his goal is to achieve happiness by going straight. But when Don Vito is shot, Michael is forced to act in novel ways. At the hospital Michael's immediate goal is to save his father, but his ultimate goal swings 180 degrees as he pledges to stand by Don Vito. Now a happy life means safeguarding his father, which means becoming an integral part of the family.

The cause-and-effect nature of this scene-by-scene action is clear. The war council scene that follows the assassination attempt makes the reverse-by-reverse nature of such action clear, too (II, 8). Michael makes the new meaning of his ultimate goal clear by setting in motion his plan to kill McCluskey and Sollozzo.

Neither Michael nor we had any reason to expect to see him involved in such behavior, but specific actions in response to specific problems force a character to show unexpected resources and to change. As characters change, they are surprised, and we through them.

Surprise, the flip side of suspense, is a critical element in a screenplay. Suspense and surprise are built into the successful handling of conflict (II, 3, 10). Michael is surprised at the hospital. His brothers are later surprised by Michael. We must be surprised too, or we will find the writing predictable and drop out. What we anticipate can happen only if its enactment exceeds our expectations and surprises us.

As his or her actions move a major character deeper into the story, a character discovers that the overall goal can be achieved only by solving a past problem, too, as we have seen (II, 11–13, and IV, 1). As this problem is overcome, both the character and the nature of the ultimate happiness that he or she envisages is irrevocably changed. Michael at the end of *The Godfather* has become the Don: the door to his study closes as his henchmen kiss his hand. Cause and-effect action leading to change, revelation, and surprise continue until the last shot.

Finally, this process of building and revealing makes characters suffer. They act because they are unhappy. Romeo and Juliet struggle and suffer to be together. Ada is in torment because her piano was abandoned in *The Piano*. Rachel faces shunning because of her love for Book in *Witness*. In *A Streetcar Named Desire* Stanley doesn't like Blanche's airs or her impact on his wife, and so he destroys her chance for a new life with Mitch, then rapes her. In *Star Wars*, Luke joins the rebellion in grief and anger over the murder of his uncle and aunt.

A suffering character opens the door to knowledge through his or her pain. Nietzsche observes that the Greek tragedians chose a handful of extreme stories from the wider range of myths available because those forced the characters to reveal their uttermost nature and capacity.[22] That drive to reveal the dimensions of human nature remains at the center of drama; suffering is the root of wisdom. Our delight in illusion transforms a character's suffering into an element of pleasure for us as he or she finally wins self-knowledge.

5. Motivation

Libraries are filled with books explaining the motivation of fictional personages like Hamlet. As we have seen, a character is always in a specific situation, facing a specific unexpected and unwanted problem or obstacle, which forces him or her to act in the name of reaching his immediate goal, simultaneously discovering and revealing motivation. Motivation is simply his or her reason for acting: it is always problem-driven and needs to be appropriate to the immediate circumstances and consistent with a given characterization. Thus we must always speak of a specific immediate motivation in response to a specific immediate problem, and we must sustain its growth reverse by reverse, just as in building a character. The two processes are inseparable.

The meaning of a character's ultimate goal and how that evolves is similarly developed. Immediate motivations, problems, and goals are related to the larger story by developing a clear relation in the plot between what is immediately and ultimately at stake in any given scene or sequence (II, 3).

In *Casablanca* both Ilse and Rick have clear, immediate goals. Ilse's immediate goal when she goes alone to Rick is to gain transit tickets for herself and her husband. Rick's immediate goal, however, is to let her know how angry and hurt he still is over her past betrayal. Rick sees his ultimate goal, his happiness, entangled with making Ilse pay for that betrayal; Ilse sees hers in escape from the Gestapo. But as Rick attacks Ilse he discovers that the truth is other than he imagined and that Ilse still loves him. Ilse discovers that for Rick's sake, she is willing to give up leaving, or to leave with him; thus she completely reverses herself. The meaning of the happiness that Ilse envisages in her ultimate goal has changed, and so has Rick's. Immediately at stake are the tickets; ultimately at stake is what Rick and Ilse will give their lives to and why. At the end of *Casablanca* we see Rick choose to let Ilse go, from love. He is going to war.

Essentially, characters are driven to discover how far they will go to reach their goals, as immediately or ultimately understood. Alexander discovers in his confrontation with the Bishop in *Fanny and Alexander* that his fear of pain limits his defiance. Rhett finds that Scarlett has gone past the limits of his endurance in *Gone with the Wind*. Cyrano wins admittance to Roxanne's bed for Christian, and actually lets Christian go to the woman that Cyrano loves in *Cyrano de Bergerac*. Pleasing Roxanne is crucial to Cyrano, even if he must suffer.

Finally, what we see of a character's motivation must also be probable in the circumstances and necessary to forward his interests. When these various requirements for building a successful character are compromised for a given character in weak writing, or in genre writing in the name of entertainment, the overall credibility of the screenplay suffers too.

VI Mind in Drama

1. Ideas and Innovation

Hollywood suffers from the notion that ideas are for academics and are inherently at odds with dramatic action and emotion. Independent and foreign films are capturing the market for meaningful drama because they are often aware that nothing is more likely to lead to action or to be felt more passionately than an idea. We are heirs to a century of "isms" that continue to drench the world with blood or, in the case of religious sects, appall and amaze us with their burning Armageddons and mass suicides.

Ideas are inescapable. They drive the heart. Reason for a character is passion married to self-serving logic. Ideas may *seem* absent or secondary to stories when they are familiar, as in 1930s song-and-dance spectacles devoted to the banal idea that love is good and true love is better. Many television shows seem just as mindless; actually, they, too, blindly assume the ideas and values prevalent in their audiences. That assumption tells a viewer *that all's right with him* and reveals the real point of such writing: ritual reassurance.

Ideas are integral to the quality of films. A spectacle like *Jurassic Park* is superior to its immediate sequel, *Jurassic Park: The Lost World*, in large part because it gives vivid enactment to the folly of scientific hubris. The sequel is reduced to holding our interest by treating a mother tyrannosaur with sympathy.

Some issues, like abortion, have topical heat. Television uses narrowly focused problem dramas, like wife-beating or alcoholism. Miniseries have fallen on hard times because since the success of *Roots,* the emphasis has been placed too often on thoughtless spectacle and weak drama with overwrought emotions.

Fresh ideas generate attention. Ibsen's *Ghosts* was the first realistic play that enjoyed major success to use a contemporary problem like syphilis to embody the idea that the sins of the father are visited on the son. It touched off a fiery reaction: "An open drain; a loathsome sore unbandaged," "Unutterably offensive," "Naked loathsomeness," "Revoltingly suggestive and blasphemous," "Garbage and offal." Ibsen was "Ugly, nasty, discordant," his admirers were "Lovers of prurience and dabblers in impropriety who are eager to gratify their illicit tastes under the pretence of art." [23]

An intimate film like *Kramer vs. Kramer* deals with the ideas that a woman needs to realize herself in some meaningful way if she is to be a good mother and that a conventional man can change and rise to a level of maternal care and sensitivity. The past and how to understand it, the nature of loyalty and truth, and the importance of conscience are central to *On The Waterfront* and *A Streetcar Named Desire. Remains of the Day* deliberately juxtaposes Stevens's refusal to think or feel beyond his butler's role with Lord Darlington's misguided political beliefs: the latter at least cares, while the former tragically emasculates himself.

Great films are married to great subjects naturally full of ideas. *Lawrence of Arabia* wrestles with the rights of a colonial people, the compromises a leader must make in order to make any progress, and the human limits of even a hero. *Fanny and Alexander* shows an ideologue in religious guise, corrupted by power and loss of faith and struggling to maintain a lie so he doesn't have to face himself—a dilemma that many agonized over in the sad twentieth century. The *Godfather* trilogy explores the validity of violence and whether family loyalty can replace all other values in a civil society. *To Kill a Mocking-*

bird examines integrity and racism. *Gone with the Wind* is at once a Civil War epic, a romance, and an exploration of social and individual resiliency and self-deception. *High Noon* affirms that a man must do what he believes to be right even if he is stripped of support, while those who give in to expediency are shown to be contemptible. Drama at its best is of both the mind and the heart.

2. Theme in Action

Ibsen's principle that action and theme must be one is basic to good screenwriting (I, 3). Ideas, theme, a screenplay's vision, must be implicit in and rise to reflection from the action. Ideas cannot be immediately at stake in the action in effective writing; they arise implicitly from the action.

Nora in Ibsen's *A Doll's House* astounded contemporary audiences by forcing her husband, Torvald, to hold a climactic, rational discussion of their marriage, rejecting his systematic arguments based on morality, religion, and convention as guides for her behavior. But what is immediately at stake is whether Torvald can keep Nora from walking out, not the abstract ins and outs of a given idea. Although the proper nature of a relationship between a man and woman ultimately rides on her choice, the scene retains an immediate, dramatic, behavioral effectiveness.

Witness builds up vividly immediate scenes that contrast the different "English" and Amish values. It strongly tilts in favor of the Amish and says that we cannot bring their values and ours together by having Book leave without Rachel. Rachel and Book do not hold a debate on the subject. She does challenge Eli, and his response is that she knows Book has to leave. They have all seen Book's violence: his action has already made the point. In this sense (only) the action is the point.

Sleepless in Seattle makes a statement in favor of risking everything for love by having the heroine break off an inappropriate relationship and take a leap on faith and hope alone. Behavior carries the message, but behavior without a message is meaningless.

3. What Structure Is For

What is plot structure? The ordering of scenes and sequences in a cause-and-effect, more or less probable and necessary manner to resolve the conflict of a dramatic story? This is true, but a superficial definition. Stories happen in our minds; what an audience attends to is an illusion of an action that reveals a particular meaning while simultaneously giving us a sense of completely understanding the characters' lives (I, 5; III, 1–2). *Plots structure the pattern of our attending, which is to say that structure communicates meaning and ends in knowledge.*

The turning point of the end of Act 1 focuses the viewer on a line of particular behavior to be pursued in Act 2 by the hero and heroine to resolve their problems, and on the inseparable meaning of that action, however further developed and complicated in Act 2 (II, 12). Act 2 tests that action and meaning. The Crisis sharply narrows the options for the protagonists a final time: now just this must be done, while how that comes out drives home the vision of the drama that has governed the selection of its incidents from the start (II, 13).

Julie resolves to live at the end of Act 1 in *Blue,* but to cut her ties to the past and be uninvolved with anyone. That resolve is systematically tested as Antoine finds her, Lucille involves her in a friendship, a family of mice must be dealt with, and Olivier finds her. Julie finds through Olivier that her husband's music was preserved against her will, that her husband had a mistress, and that Olivier is completing a composition of her husband's. Julie turns on Olivier angrily in the Crisis, but he tells her he will do anything to make her live fully again. To live she must face her past and be with others. Her Act 1 resolve has failed, its meaning been explored and confounded. The Crisis clearly points the choice facing her definitively in Act 3.

Lisa joins Jeff at the end of Act 1 in *Rear Window* in pursuing a murderer. Act 2 tests that pursuit, but when Doyle fails to come up with evidence, their decent behavior is made to look like meddling. They give up briefly in the Crisis, until a neighbor's grief over her murdered dog rekindles their drive in specific terms: good neighbors do care about each other, and so Lisa and Jeff resume their efforts on their own. The connection between meaning and action is transparent, while the Crisis not only points out a definitive line of action but does so in a specific framework of meaning.

Dave decides to take action at the end of Act 1 in *Dave* to save the bill wanted by his "wife," meaning: integrity matters and may be the road to respect and love. Act 2 challenges that resolve, as first the president's wife discovers Dave's true identity, and they both almost leave before resolving to work together. Then they are brought to an impossible point in the Crisis as Bob strikes back with charges that are true of the president but not of Dave. Dave first runs in the Crisis, but, with the president's wife, resolves to strike back. This clearly sets up our expectation that Act 3 must resolve this issue and through its action show a path that combines the possibility for real love and integrity.

Emilie and the Bishop after their marriage at the end of Act 1 in *Fanny and Alexander* walk off with the children to a world that Emilie thinks possesses purity and truth. Act 2 systematically tests that belief, and in the Crisis leaves the beaten Alexander in Emilie's arms in mutual despair in the attic. The action shows that Emilie has been wrong about the Bishop and what life with him means. The content of Act 3 is clearly presaged: escaping and finding something truer. No one says that middle-class values are truer in the End; Gustav Adolf is deprecatory about the Ekdahls' understanding of larger historical issues. But Emilie and Alexander are clearly happier, and by making a worldly gathering the final action, Bergman communicates his vision as clearly as Kieslowski and Piesiewicz in *Blue* or Wallace and Kelly in *Witness*.

Structure in effective screenwriting is transparent: analysis always makes things too schematic. We do not sit in the audience thinking, "Aha! Act 1 turning point! This means . . . or "Voila! The Crisis! I should expect issue *x* to be dealt with in the following way . . ." Effective writing places the audience in the characters' state of immediate, desperate ignorance. The Act 1 turning point is a discovery, the best choice available in a swift flow of surprising incidents. Act 2 tests a similar series of unexpected and unwanted developments, while its Crisis is a decisive turn at once surprising and inevitable, if it is well written. We experience everything through our identification with the characters, without knowing until the last moment how it will end and what that finally means. Later, when we reflect on how thoroughly that involvement and its meaning were guided, we are surprised.

A certain sign of bad writing is our awareness of the structure and our ability to predict the action.

4. Creating Values and Moral Urgency

Here is a passage chosen at random from *Fanny and Alexander*. The Bishop (Edvard) and Emilie have just retired in the evening; earlier the Bishop had beaten Alexander.

EMILIE

You're crazy.

EDVARD

(smiling)

I must confess I find you least attractive when you make an effort to be vulgar. As I said, there are one or two things I could ask about, but I don't want to pick a quarrel, so I'll hold my peace.

EMILIE

You lock the children in.

EDVARD

A safety measure, Emilie. I wanted a guarantee that you would come back.

EMILIE

You ill-treated Alexander.

EDVARD

You express yourself so dramatically, dear Emilie. I punished him. That is part of my duty in bringing him up. Moreover, the punishment was mild in relation to the crime.

EMILIE

He is bleeding and the skin has been stripped off.[24]

They are warring over values, over two versions of the truth and reality. Emilie claims that Edvard's behavior was wrong because it was excessive, leading him into a cruel absurdity. Edvard asserts his right to discipline a child and reproaches Emilie for being melodramatic and so untrustworthy that he has to lock up the children so she will stay. Underlying this is Edvard's terror of being wrong: he is willing to use force to prevent being proven wrong.

This is typical: characters are always in conflict over what means to use to gain their goals, or what means are being used against them, and whether those are right or wrong. This affirming or denying of values is inescapable in screenwriting. As we saw above, even such light entertainment as much of television writing reassuringly affirms prevailing values. A screenplay inevitably affirms some values while spurning others as wrong, even evil.

Moral urgency flows from this feature of dramatic writing. Pursuing the murderer matters tremendously to Jeff and Lisa in *Rear Window;* finding a meaningful life matters enormously to Dave in *Dave;* working things out with Roxanne is the most important thing in his life to Charlie in *Roxanne.* Public as well as private regeneration depends on Terry's leading the longshoremen into work at the end of *On the Waterfront;* having any kind of meaningful existence rides on Blanche's efforts to win a second chance in *A Streetcar Named Desire;* Julie is enraged by being forced to live on Olivier's terms in *Blue.*

Since ultimately the survival of the main characters that we identify with is at stake, one way or another, as defined in given stories, whatever values they affirm as right or deny as wrong feel equally urgent to us in successful writing.

It does not follow from this that writers are moralists or that they write with a consistent ethical outlook film by film. A story that recommends a reasoned hedonism, like *Fanny and Alexander,* may be followed by one with quite another message. A good deal of Bergman's early work does not presage the vision in *Fanny and Alexander.*

It does follow that an effective film without moral urgency is almost inconceivable—even in farces the outcome matters intensely to the protagonists. What would be left to a film whose characters don't care what happens? A screenwriter, then, cannot escape this aspect of the art. His art can be abused easily, as in propaganda films, because of its immediate, value-rich impact on an audience. He has a responsibility to write well, with force and point, and to consider just what it is that he makes an audience feel with passion. His endeavor is embedded in the society in which he lives, and his stature is rooted in his ability to influence other lives.

VII Spectacle and Other Elements

1. Spectacle and Special Effects

                    Spectacle has a profound impact on us. Paleolithic caves provided spectacular settings for art and whatever rites they may have housed, as do the great cathedrals, while the images of Nazi torchlight parades or May Day parades through Red Square are emblematic of the twentieth century. The March on Washington climaxed by Martin Luther King Jr.'s "I Have a Dream" speech was a great spectacle. Raging floods or fires or man-made spectaculars like the opening ceremonies of the Olympics rivet us. Our summer vacations often return us to the nature our forebears lived in harmony with before the rise of consciousness made them men. Even now a notable sunset lets us touch our lost innocence for an awed moment. Spectacle, like music, can sweep away our sense of individuality for a joyous moment of communal (admirable or not) or natural wholeness.

    Use of spectacle in drama is as old as the Greeks, who called for flying chariots, gods to drop in from heaven, and earthquakes. But film greatly expands the scope and verisimilitude of spectacle in drama; many of Hollywood's great dramas are equally great spectacles, like *Gone with the Wind*. Often the studios are so obsessed with spectacle and special effects that their films prove to be artistic and financial embarrassments because of their dramatic weakness. "The play's the thing" is a lesson that they have still to learn.

Some films not normally regarded as spectacles actually are spectacles, like *Kramer vs. Kramer;* its New York scenes are spectacles in Wyoming or Calcutta. All of our films are spectacular, given their larger-than-life projection (I, 4); however, we typically use "spectacle" to refer to mass action or an unusually scenic element.

Screenwriters make various uses of this powerful tool. The waterfront and gritty tenement shots establish the setting for *On the Waterfront.* The image of Kane standing alone in an empty street in the midday glare in the Crisis of *High Noon* powerfully evokes emotion, as does the famous Odessa Steps sequence of *The Battleship Potemkin.* The latter does so by using a mass spectacle. The climbing sequences create anticipation in *For Your Eyes Only* and *The Eiger Sanction,* as does Dunbar's ride over the rolling plains looking for the Sioux village in *Dances with Wolves.*

Landscape, starscape in science fiction, and urban vistas have various additional roles beyond establishing settings. *Shane* uses western spectacle as a stage for warring visions, as do *The Emerald Forest* and *Medicine Man* with jungle settings. Landscape—here the Rockies—is idealized in *Jeremiah Johnson* as the place free of mud and people where an unspoiled life is possible. *Unforgiven* and *High Plains Drifter* use their unspoiled landscapes to isolate morality. Space is a place of symbolic possibility where we illumine our capacities in the *Star Trek* films; *The Last of the Mohicans* uses landscape to evoke the possibility of a free, natural life. *Never Cry Wolf* combines natural and mass spectacles in a caribou hunt by wolves to dramatize a man's return to nature. The setting of *The Big Easy* is exotic and emblematic of a lifestyle, while the often claustrophobic settings of murder mysteries or film noir evoke a world of moral ambiguity typical of urban life.

But no doubt the most common use of spectacle is as pure entertainment, like the famous opening of *Star Wars. Jurassic Park* and its offspring are also entertainments, as are the spectacular routines of 1930s dance movies, or genre action sequences (IV, 4).

The spaceships of *Star Wars* or the dinosaurs of *Jurassic Park* are also special effects, largely computer-generated. A Jedi's weapon is a special effect. Realistic films are full of special effects, like gunfire, the accident in *Blue*, and the murder in *Witness*.

Spectacle and special effects cannot carry a drama in themselves. Once past the simple use of establishing a setting, spectacle and special effects must be fused with our emotional involvement. Even *Star Wars* emphasizes the human importance of its spectacle and special effects. These, like the Death Star, gain importance and meaning because of what they represent to the people we care for. Films with weak characters vanish swiftly, whatever their spectacle.

2. Music and Sound Effects

Music drama has remained a major goal of dramatists since opera developed during the Renaissance as an attempt to revive Greek drama. Musicals are an established film genre, whether in the classic Rodgers and Hammerstein variety or in modern musicals like *Hair* or *Rent* or in musical films like *The Commitments*. Some films seem to be made for the sake of their sound tracks.

We take a musical score for granted in virtually all films: its absence comes as a surprise in Bergman's films, or in a film like *King Solomon's Mines*. Music has such emotional power that it has long stood on its own and has often been regarded as more fundamental and direct in its appeal than drama. Nietzsche derived Greek tragedy from music, while we know its ability to transport us whether through a classical or popular variant, as a rock concert. Allied with a script, music underscores the dramatic force of the action—or hides its weakness through its own depth. For this reason a libretto appears to be a mere sketch staged on its own, a story of great power performed in its musical context.

Obvious uses of music in films include using it to link one scene with another. Leitmotifs presage the appearance of a character, like the shark in *Jaws*. Music can establish or change a mood, whether intimate or epic, threatening or reassuring. The score gives the pastoral scenes of the Amish a magical appeal at the start of *Witness*, while its edginess underscores the danger of the night when Joey is killed in *On the Waterfront*. Music heightens the celebration at the end of *Star Wars* with its overwhelming fanfare: in *Alien* it constantly increases the tension. Some thematic music is so distinctive that it gives a film a memorable character in itself, as in *The Godfather, Out of Africa, Star Wars,* or *Rocky.*

Music can be used ironically, too, as in comedy, where a solemn occasion and music can be made absurd by the antics of a character, like the new minister in *Four Weddings and a Funeral.* In *Schindler's List* classical music is used to obscure the horror of a barbaric "health" selection process in the work camp. A love song presages murders in *Sea of Love,* and so on.

These traditional uses of music become travesties when music is used tritely or props up a weak script. But music intimately bound to effective dramatic writing and spectacle gives some scenes a dynamic impact not otherwise attainable, like Terry's climactic walk in *On the Waterfront,* the salt works confrontation or the walk to the sea in *Gandhi,* the siege and Ichimonji's descent from the burning castle in *Ran,* or Nobunaga's lament in *Kagemusha.*

Sometimes music is a distraction. Orchestras seem to be hidden in every tangle of jungle in *The Emerald Forest* and behind every dune in *Lawrence of Arabia.* Some scores merely deafen. Screenwriters like Bergman have shown that films with minimal scores filled with natural sounds are just as capable of producing powerful drama.

A screenwriter does not write the score. But music remains a powerful tool for him too. Any musical effect integral to the dramatic action is his to demand or write in. He can use a particular song or music, like jazz, to establish or change moods, as in *Bird;* to presage action, as in *Sea of Love* or in *Witness,* where a specific "golden oldie" creates the opportunity for Book to take Rachel into his arms for a dance. A screenwriter can call for specific music to define characters or opportunities, or evoke the past, like communicating Blanche's tenuous hold on reality by the use of the Varsouviana Waltz, which only she hears, in *A Streetcar Named Desire.*

The very rhythm of the action and images is an instinctive musical (rhythmic) element that a screenwriter creates (I, 4). Effectively structuring the pace of the action and emphasizing its movement in climactic moments is integral to effective writing, not just something that is added in an editing booth. Good writers master this underlying sense of rhythm that is more important than more obviously musical elements.

A screenwriter can also call for unmusical sound effects, like the whistle that drowns out the action as Terry repeats information to Edie that we already know in *On the Waterfront*. He can call for steps to be heard, or gunshots, typical city or pastoral sounds, explosions, love cries, or silence.

3. Dialogue

A screenwriter writes an action, a story based on conflicted behavior, not just words. Action sequences largely dispense with dialogue, as do some of the most effective dramatic moments in films, like Rachel offering herself to Book in *Witness*, Mitch examining Blanche's face in the light in *A Streetcar Named Desire*, Terry discovering his brother's body in *On the Waterfront*, or Alan seeing his first dinosaur in *Jurassic Park*. Words should never be used when behavior communicates the meaning.

This said, dialogue remains our primary tool.

The prevalent dialogue style has been our everyday, conversational idiom since the theatrical revolution at the end of the nineteenth century (I, 3). We expect characters to speak that way whether their lives are contemporary, historical, or long ago in another galaxy.

Dialogue must be appropriate to character. We don't expect Rachel to curse in *Witness*, while Book's dialogue is naturally more colorful. Dialogue should characterize, as with Blanche's poetically charged lines counterpoised against Mitch's literal and prosaic expressions in *A Streetcar Named Desire*. Kujan's language is accusatory, demanding, imperative, and mocking in *The Usual Suspects*, while Verbal's is defensive, hesitant, reluctant. Dialogue must be consistent: Verbal can't start talking like a cowboy; Terry in *On the Waterfront* can't suddenly talk like a professor.

Screen dialogue must be economical. Even poetic, charged screen dialogue is spare compared to similar passages on the legitimate stage. There language must be used to evoke the meaning and emotion that the camera can show powerfully through nuance and gesture in properly constructed conflict (I, 4). Even merely heightened dialogue runs the risk of seeming stilted to our democratic ears.

Above all, dialogue expresses emotion. Look again at the passage from *Fanny and Alexander* in VI, 4. What leaps out beyond the terms of their argument is the depth of Emilie's anger and hurt, discernible from her pointed, direct lines, and the Bishop's attempt to excuse himself in lines that give the impression of words flung against the truth. Moreover, Emilie's feelings prepare us for the subsequent rescue of the children. Feelings revealed by dialogue lead to action.

Dialogue has always primarily conveyed emotion: Oedipus in *Oedipus Rex* reassures the chorus because he both needs and wants to calm their fears. The expressions of intention, response, situation, and exposition are all in the service of emotion. This is the point of the observation in II, 7 that giving information in a scene must be immediately motivated. Book is full of emotional urgency and desire in order to convince Schaefer to act against McFee in *Witness*. The Schofield Kid tells Munny the amplified story about the slashed whore in *Unforgiven* because he wants his help in getting the reward. Everything Verbal reveals is motivated by his desire to get out of Kujan's office in *The Usual Suspects*.

Motivation is desire, and dialogue is its expression.

What is a character's ultimate desire? To end conflict and achieve happiness, however that is envisioned.

Sometimes dialect is called for, which requires a writer to familiarize himself or herself with a given idiom. It is better for dialogue to suggest dialect with a few choice expressions if there is to be a lot of it, rather than to flesh it out word by word academically. The audience gets the point and is able to follow the sense more easily.

Teleplays sometimes use curtain lines for each commercial break, or "act," a line designed to provide a bridge that can be remembered until the action resumes. Scenes may use tag lines in the same way, but with immediate consequences, as in the frequent farewells that villains make to James Bond, thinking they are sending him off to execution. These are old devices—Shakespeare routinely used such lines.

Weak or new writers make a number of common dialogue errors. Speaking without conversational contractions is stilted, using two or more words where fewer will do is talky. Directing lines by specifying their emotional content when that is obvious, like anger or grief, signals inexperience. Characters who make speeches instead of swiftly reacting to one another flout our sense of conversational realism. Only special circumstances justify speeches, as when Terry takes on Johnny Friendly in the climax of *On the Waterfront*, or the Bishop reviews punishments to break Alexander's will in *Fanny and Alexander*. A speech, like an effective song or soliloquy, must be an action in itself.

Finally, notwithstanding anything above, when deep passion is expressed in great language it has the force of music and can sweep characters away, and us with them. Romeo at Juliet's balcony, Hamlet soliloquizing, Charlie in *Roxanne* writing beautiful letters or wooing Roxanne for Chris significantly deepens the emotional impact and pleasure of the action. We thrill to such language when it is dramatically motivated. Comedy often emphasizes wit, like the funny, pithy exchanges in *Much Ado About Nothing* or *Four Weddings and a Funeral:* these would fall flat if reduced to prosaic dialogue. Cyrano dazzles as he extemporizes a poem in rhyming couplets while dueling in *Cyrano de Bergerac.*

Even Terry, recent bum and ex-fighter with little verbal skill, is fired by passion to a charged language appropriate to the docks as he dares the longshoremen to see Friendly as their betrayer in *On the Waterfront.* Munny's dialogue is often deliberately repetitive and prosaic in a comedic way as he tries to reassure himself he is no longer a soulless killer in *Unforgiven,* but when the Schofield Kid in the Crisis reflects that the man he killed had it coming, Munny has the powerful rejoinder: "We all have it coming, kid." A W. H. Auden poem is recited with deep affect in the funeral oration of *Four Weddings and a Funeral;* Karen makes an equally charged use of poetry in *Out of Africa* at Finch Hatten's funeral.

Poetic expressiveness is as natural to us as plastic representation and telling stories: we stunt our humanity when we deny our ability to use the charged, expressive language that communicates passion in its transcendent moments, or in its wittiness lets us laugh at folly and tragedy.

4. Symbol and Metaphor

Our ability to think and interact symbolically is central to our evolution into humanity. Language is deeply symbolic, and our ability to tell and enjoy stories, including screenplays, is a function of this innate ability to create symbolic realities. We are the symbolic species.

Screenplays are symbolic language in the form of an illusory imitation of an action: that is, a metaphor, a likening of one thing to another, of an imaginary conception to reality. We are confident that such "metaphors" can be profitable, can move, educate, relieve, and divert us. The amusing "rescue" by the Maoris in *The Piano* is a good reminder of how symbol-making is universal but specific symbol systems are culture-bound and learned (I, 2, 5).

Symbols abound. Think of those for male or female, the dollar sign, the swastika, the flag, and Uncle Sam. Whether the last two are burned or dragged through the streets are matters that remain controversial. A hero rides a white horse; a clerical collar symbolizes a way of life. Environmentalists, Republicans, and Democrats have their symbols, as do NOW, the Gaullists in France, Marxists anywhere. Each of the physical elements has its symbol, while the signs of the zodiac symbolize personality types. Our mental life would be impossible without symbolic thought processes.

Symbols can speak to us as directly and powerfully as music, forcefully moving the action forward, giving a story a deep grasp on our underlying emotions. They communicate crucial information economically and often give or buttress key elements of characterization. Archetypal patterns are symbolic: the hero symbolizes our hoped-for capacity to overcome great odds; the Pygmalion story, whether *La Femme Nikita* or *My Fair Lady,* suggests an almost unlimited hope in the power of individual transformation (I, 2).

Symbols are either specific elements or symbolic actions within screenplays. They can be borrowed from life, or they can develop uniquely. The .44 Magnum that Dirty Harry carries is symbolic of his potency as an enforcer; the sword that a samurai treasures demonstrates his status. The western hero usually is on a white horse. Kane symbolically throws his badge in the dust in *High Noon.* Lisa's gown at her entrance in *Rear Window* marks her unsuitability as the wife of a photographer who is often in wild places.

Symbols, like music, can be used ironically, too. The western hero in Eastwood's *Pale Rider* first appears wearing a clerical collar that he removes later in the action when he gets his guns. A prostitute in *Two Mules for Sister Sara* wears a nun's habit. These variants are forms of irony (see 5, below).

Symbolic actions include Book's indicating his imminent departure when just before the Crisis he remounts the birdcage he destroyed on his arrival at the Lapps' home in *Witness.* Terry's cargo hook is his tool of trade in *On the Waterfront;* his playing with it as Edie begs him to leave is a symbolic action, as is his donning Joey's jacket, which has come to stand for "the reformer" as he leaves to go demand his rights. His walk into the warehouse carries the symbolic meaning of taking over the union. Munny in Act 3 of *Unforgiven* begins drinking, a symbolic action that tells us he is reverting to the kind of killer he used to be. Rachel senses Book watching her as she bathes, and turns to him; we understand her action to be an offer.

These are powerful writing resources. A screenwriter will be aware of some from the start; other symbolic elements and actions must be refined as they become evident in revision in their particular and unique emergence in a given story.

5. Dramatic Irony

Dramatic irony is almost as widespread as symbol, and as deeply embedded in our innate abilities. We have been ironic since we have been social. Irony at its simplest is understatement, an appearance of detachment that belies the facts. It can seem sardonic, leading to bitter or cynical expressions. As a figure of speech, it represents a deliberate reversal of meaning, as when a character says, "I love this guy," but means the opposite.

Reversal of meaning is always at the heart of irony.

Dramatic action that becomes ironic can generate great emotional weight. The classic way of understanding dramatic irony is as a situation where the audience has knowledge that none—or very few—characters possess. *Oedipus Rex* is the classic example: we know Oedipus is the man he is searching for. A dramatist shifts our focus by using knowledge in this way from the outcome of a story to how an expected outcome will take shape.

More typically, the audience knows something that one of the main characters doesn't know, but that one or more do. The climactic scene between Terri and Nicolai in *An Affair to Remember* works this way. We know what happened to Terri, as do other characters, but Nicolai does not. The tension in the scene builds around whether he will finally discover the truth. An otherwise weak film ends strongly when he does.

This scene simultaneously shows another variant of dramatic irony, where one character knowingly uses it against another. The audience must know the truth for this to work. Terri, unsure whether Nicolai was present at the top of the Empire State Building, lets him manipulate her into pretending she was there and not him; as he reveals the details of waiting for her, she poignantly realizes the truth.

Finally, a character may know the truth, which neither the audience nor other characters know until later, perhaps not even until the end. Mrs. Mulwray in *Chinatown* uses irony in this way, withholding key information concerning incest from Gittes and the audience, information that both discover with a sense of horror in the Crisis.

Captain Schaefer in *Witness* withholds his knowledge from Book and the audience until McFee's assassination attempt gives him away near the end of Act 1. Verbal, in *The Usual Suspects*, beguiles all until the end. The truth revealed is always the opposite of the truth initially imagined. Dramatic irony drives home our limited, fallible nature and underscores the ignorance with which we and characters must deal. We can never know all there is to know and must always be subject to surprise. Irony as a dramatic tool is a scalpel that lays bare our presumptions, vanities, and ignorance with unusual elegance, so we delight in the process, however the characters may suffer.

6. Comedic Turns

Comedy is a specialized field abounding in specialist manuals, but certain basic observations belong here. All dramatists utilize the same underlying dramatic structure that we have reviewed, although some are innately comic, others serious. A comic screenwriter has a defining angle of vision that sees the human situation as absurd or ludicrous, while a "serious" dramatist sees our more or less tragic nature, however happy the final outcome of a given story. Often the one cannot see the perspective of the other.

The comic angle of vision first manifests itself in the premise. The story pattern envisioned usually shows a progression from unhappiness to happiness on the part of the main characters (II, 6; IV, 4). A comic dramatist doesn't imagine the devil in disguise trying to get out of a police station, as in *The Usual Suspects*, but a frustrated actor saving his career by impersonating a woman and then falling in love with the woman in his life, as in *Tootsie*. Or he imagines a man with too long a nose helping an idiot win the woman he loves in *Roxanne*, not the star-crossed young lovers of *Romeo and Juliet*.

Comic stories make great use of three particular plot stratagems in carrying out their premises: reversal of expectation, piling on complications, and flirting with tragedy.

Reversal of expectation has broad variations. In one, a screenwriter creates a particular expectation and satisfies it unexpectedly: for example, we expect to see a particular adulterous couple in bed if a door opens but discover another adulterous couple when it does. Or a screenwriter may reverse expected behavior, as when Roxanne and Charlie argue over who is to get in and who out of her house after their confrontation over his misleading letters.

Piling on complications is a favorite technique. Michael, in *Tootsie*, can't find work, so he pretends to be a woman. That woman's success becomes a problem: "she" is in demand. "She" becomes Julie's confidante and advises Julie about the men she is dating, then falls in love with her. Julie's father falls in love with Tootsie and proposes. Dilemmas turn amusing if too many pile up: soon we are laughing at the absurd nature of experience lived through these characters, fulfilling the comic screenwriter's vision.

Our most substantial comedies flirt with tragedy, ranging from moments of serious misunderstanding or pathos in the Crisis to a deliberate evocation of tragic possibility, for the Crisis inevitably creates a prospect of imminent failure in all drama. Michael in *Tootsie* finally can't take it anymore and dramatically disrobes, ruining his career as Tootsie and endangering his relationship with the shocked Julie. Sydney angrily leaves Andrew in *The American President* when he plays politics with "her" bill. Roxanne is incensed at Charlie in *Roxanne* for his deception. Dave appears to have a heart attack in *Dave*. The ensuing happy endings feel happier for having survived these brushes with failure.

Branagh's version of *Much Ado About Nothing* brings out Shakespeare's powerful use of this technique through Claudio's vivid denunciation of Hero at their wedding ceremony (reversed expectation), leaving her distraught and dishonored and her father outraged. The comic angle of vision disappears despite our knowing that the underlying plot to deceive Claudio has been exposed (dramatic irony), for none of the principals knows that yet. The door is thus left open to tragedy, but it is swiftly shut and the comedy resumed. Bergman uses the same technique in *Smiles of a Summer Night* as Count Malcolm challenges Egerman to play Russian roulette. We hear a shot, and we don't know for a moment whether Egerman is alive. Then he appears with his face farcically blackened by smoke—the bullet was a blank.

Flirting with tragedy draws attention to the illusory nature of comedic action: for a moment we sense that just under comedy's giddy surface life is, after all, inescapably tragic. That realization gives the action a poignant pleasure when the comedy resumes and a happy ending ensues.

Not all comedies flirt with tragedy. In many the Crisis only provides for heightened laughter. It is a fundamental divide in the genre. Who experiences the pathos in such films provides the clue for their difference. In films like *The Gold Rush* or *Roxanne* or *Much Ado About Nothing*, it is we who are expected to experience the characters' feelings; in films like *One, Two, Three* or those by the Marx Brothers, Laurel and Hardy, or Abbott and Costello only the characters are expected to feel pathos.

The first variety of comedy lays bare the illusory nature of the hilarious action through our brief encounter with the human condition in its pathetic or tragic dimension. The second variety catches us up in the illusion that we are free from the tragic condition or that that condition is not tragic after all, as we watch the characters in such a story deal seriously with ever greater absurdities. It is impossible to take either character or situation seriously in such a context. Here we identify with the comic perspective itself: we ask only that the incidents confirm it.

Both forms of comedy make experience tolerable through their different use of the illusion of the action. The first inevitably tends toward serious drama, the latter toward farce. Many films, like *Roxanne* and *Dave*, mingle these perspectives initially, before settling into one or the other. Steve Martin, like Shakespeare, typically weaves ongoing strands of farce through more substantial stories, whether as the fireman of *Roxanne* or Bottom and his cohorts in *A Midsummer Night's Dream*.

A number of other techniques are commonplace in comedy. One is verbal misconstruction, as when Roxanne and Charlie briefly argue over the pronunciation of a sentence in which she thought she heard "earn more sessions by shaving" while he was saying something entirely different.

Another favorite is reductio ad absurdum. In *Roxanne* Chris hides a radio link under an absurd cap so he can repeat lines to Roxanne that Charlie whispers from another location. Chris is reduced to police alerts and weather forecasts when the connection suffers interference. Billie, in *Born Yesterday*, sets the first ten amendments to a Christmas carol and sings them in company. A morbid turn is taken in *Fargo* when the killer is discovered pushing a leg into a wood shredder.

Mistaken identity can have tragic repercussions, as in *Donnie Brasco* or *Hamlet*, but it is always funny in comedy. Julie's father, holding Tootsie, proposes; Roxanne believes that Chris has Charlie's soul. The technique has been used since the Greeks, has famous variations in Shakespeare's *Twelfth Night* and *A Midsummer Night's Dream*, and is important in *Some Like It Hot*, *Victor/Victoria*, and *The Birdcage*, as well as many more.

All forms of dramatic irony with their implied reversals work well in comedy too, particularly in the form of one character's having something crucial that he or she withholds from others (see 5, above). *Tootsie* is deeply ironic in this sense, while all cases of mistaken identity lend themselves to such a use, whether in *The Birdcage* or Shakespeare's comedies. The simplest use of dramatic irony as a figure of speech, saying one thing while meaning another, is endemic in comedic dialogue. When Charlie first meets Roxanne, naked and locked out of her house, he doesn't offer her anything when she ironically says she is fine.

Physical comedy is a staple of comedy, whether in the form of pratfalls, pie-in-the-face routines, ridiculous details, bizarre costuming, or exaggerated forms of behavior or patterns of speech. *The Graduate* makes hay of Ben in the pool with his diving gifts, *Roxanne* ridicules Charlie's nose; *The Birdcage* exaggerates and parodies gender behavior and speech, *Mrs. Doubtfire* uses exaggerated costuming, and sets some of it on fire. The Little Tramp unbalances the cabin overhanging a precipice in *The Gold Rush* as he scurries back and forth; Munny in *Unforgiven* gets a shotgun to hit a target that he's missed with a pistol. We are simpler than we think, and we love even the most obvious devices, like slipping on a banana peel, that unravel our pretensions.

These latter techniques are another way toward farce, as well as the different use of identification in films that don't flirt with tragedy (see above), and are typified by broad exaggeration in practice. Characters can pursue reasonable ends absurdly or absurd ends reasonably— both courses of action lead to broad effects. *Roxanne* employs both: one moment we see a fireman aloft on a stream of water in a training exercise, the next we see Charlie using a radio connection to help Chris with Roxanne. *Roxanne* uneasily mixes romantic comedy and farce as Charlie writes beautiful love letters, then humiliates his firemen as he rescues a cat. *Dave* starts off farcically as Dave rides a pig to advertise Chevrolets, then settles into political satire and romantic comedy. Egerman's blackened face is an element of farce in *Smiles of a Summer Night,* but the preceding Russian roulette is menacing. Mixing these elements is commonplace, an element of taste that has become universal.

The standard of necessary and probable takes on a particular coloration in comedy. The need for plot incidents to be necessary is unchanged, but probability is used to lead us into absurdity. An effective comic screenwriter is especially careful to establish character and conflict to give us an emotionally viable norm from which the action develops, no matter how imaginative the first steps a character takes may be, as with Michael in *Tootsie.* Once the audience is hooked, a comic screenwriter uses cause-and-effect action to make later situations seem logical, however improbable. That comic use of cause-and-effect action structurally exemplifies the comic angle of vision.

7. Adaptation

Frequently a film is an adaptation of a work from another medium, sometimes from a play, as in *A Man for All Seasons* or *Frankie and Johnny,* but more usually from a novel, like *Gone with the Wind* or *Dr. Zhivago.* Although adaptation, like comedic writing, is a specialized field with its own array of manuals, certain observations apply here too.

First, a screenwriter must decide whether a work has dramatic possibility, or is really effective only in its original medium. A screenwriter has to remember that the final version of an adaptation must work as a screenplay. Second, a screenwriter must acquire the rights to adapt a particular work through negotiating with the publisher, agent, or writer. Many less-well-known writers will permit adaptations on speculation at little or no cost.

Making an adaptation involves a number of specific principles. Typically the adapted work is a novel, which means contracting its story to fit within a screenplay's Running Time and to make coherent sense in Dramatic Time (III, 3). A novel's narrative action must be translated into immediate, dramatic action between the central characters in response to defined problems, with any necessary information or backstory emerging in the ways already reviewed in II–VII.

To accomplish such a transition, a screenwriter must first summarize the work clearly. Then he must decide what the point is and which action is essential for its dramatization. He is free to do whatever is dramatically necessary while being guided by the original intent and spirit of the work. That is what stirred the screenwriter's imagination initially, and what must be communicated on the screen. Any story elements that don't directly bear on these tasks are expendable, whether they be character, plot, or theme.

Sometimes action must be invented where it is only alluded to in a literary fashion in the novel if that is necessary to create a coherent cause-and-effect sequence of action. Sometimes several characters must be merged into a single character, instead of cutting all of a particular variety or function. More rarely, characters must be added to dramatize essential action. Dramatic dialogue must replace novelistic dialogue because the original dialogue wasn't written according to the constraints that guide contemporary screenplay dialogue, and thus sounds false when spoken. Hemingway's dialogue is a particular trap in this regard.

Dune provides a good example of pitfalls to avoid. The story works best as a novel because many elements are better left to the imagination, like Baron Harkonnen's skin disease. Key parts of the action are dependent on telepathic effects or internal reflection, elements for which narration is an awkward, intrusive substitute. The action stays too close to the novel, though it reduces the novel to a Running Time of two hours and forty minutes; the result is that narration is called on further to explain otherwise cryptic action, yet it is never able to fill in enough without becoming novelistic. Characters who are interesting in the novel, where there is time and space to meet them, confuse the viewer in the film because they are not reduced to manageable numbers or introduced properly. The point of the story inevitably remains obscure.

Sometimes narration can be used as an additional stylistic element, as in *A River Runs Through It*, but narration cannot substitute for action (IV, 4). Anyone who is familiar with MacLean's novella will immediately realize that adapting a play or short work of fiction involves considerable expansion on the screenwriter's part. In order to write a full dramatic action, he or she must summarize and evaluate as with a longer work, but then must develop action and characters to fill out the action that is missing from such works or only suggested.

A great deal of the past only briefly alluded to is dramatized in the beginning of *A River Runs Through It. A Man for All Seasons* is greatly expanded in the film made from the play: the action of non-Shakespearean plays rarely translates easily to the screen. The Common Man and his narrative is dropped; all the action is dramatized onscreen, and spectacular effects are added, like the king's arrival by barge at More's and More's trial. *Frankie and Johnny* is similarly expanded into an urban framework until the end, where it stays too close to the original and becomes static and talky.

VIII Developing and Filming the Story

1. How Stories Really Develop

Screenplays start with a glimmer of vision seen darkly through the glass of the imagination. Characters or conflict or theme may suggest themselves from limitless directions (II, 2–3; V, 1), but such elements are *developed* through revision as a screenwriter explores his material, including the larger, fundamental story pattern in which the immediate drama takes root (I, 1).

There are as many ways of developing a story as there are screenwriters, each approach judged by its individual usefulness. Some writers use a premise and treatment (see 2, below). Some do all the work in their heads before writing, others use legal pads to jot down and refine ideas for plot, character, conflict, and meaning in whatever order they occur until they are ready to start. Some use index cards for each scene or sequence, dropping or adding as seems right, testing the order. Some operate by free-associating, note after note, and let their spouses highlight seemingly related elements, which they then turn into meaningful sequences. Some take an initial idea and go directly to a rough draft, finding their way scene by scene. Some resort to magical devices, as did Ibsen, who reportedly placed troll statuettes on his desk in proportion to the difficulty of creating or revising a scene.

Formulating a *provisional* premise, as reviewed in II, 6, gives a screenwriter an initial grip on the material. A number of questions further help a screenwriter clarify the screenplay: At any given moment, who is there? Why? Where and when is "there"? What are the characters doing? What is their problem? Why can't they solve it right away? What do they do next? What point of view, what vision, what theme, is suggested by this action?

Why start here and not elsewhere (II, 5–6; IV, 1)? Why *now*? What crucial event happens that draws the past into the present and requires that both be resolved together? What is the past problem? How are the fates of the protagonists linked (II, 11)? Who is the antagonist? What additional surprising complications are there? What cause-and-effect sequence leads the characters from one step to the next? Is each step necessary and probable (III, 6)? Does each contribute to our understanding of the screenplay's point?

What turning point concludes Act 1 and directs the action to be pursued in Act 2? Is it a defined moment or a sequence? What is that action pursued in Act 2? What additional characters, or surprising complications, are there? What is the Crisis at which the line of action pursued in Act 2 seems to or actually does fail (II, 12)? How does that tightly focus the climactic action for Act 3? Do the main characters succeed in Act 3? What do they reveal of themselves *definitively* then (II, 13)?

How is the past laid to rest? What point (vision, theme) is communicated by the way the story actually ends? Did the Act 1 turning point prepare us for that meaning? Did the Crisis force the conflict to take a clarifying, revelatory turn that made the dramatization of that meaning inevitable (VI, 2)? Remember, structure and meaning are inseparable (VI, 3).

Often a screenwriter reaches a stage of frustration in revision that feels like he is butting his head against a wall: if he perseveres at this point, his story has a chance to reach real cohesion. Half a year to two years after beginning, the screenplay finally presents itself with an air of clarity and ease.

2. Premise, Treatment, Stepsheet, Storyboard

Many writers use a standard premise and treatment to develop their ideas; new writers need to master these forms in order to submit proposals. Most writers in television use these forms routinely.

The premise may be interpreted in either of two ways. In the first, it is a brief statement giving the essential conflict and point of a story that has been previously reviewed. In the second, a premise, or idea, is a two- or three-page presentation of a proposed story, always typed double-spaced and largely in the present tense to give the sense of prospective action. Think of the premise as having four sections. The first sums up the entire story and its point; the second introduces the action and main characters and takes them through Act 1, clearly showing the crucial turning point at the end of that act; the third carries the characters and action to the Crisis at the end of Act 2, showing any new complications and developments; the last carries the action through the Climax (and resolution) of Act 3, clearly showing how the story's point is driven home. Such narration is summary, spending little time on individual scenes or sequences, concentrating instead on communicating the essential story line and interest of the drama.

A treatment is a much more substantial form. It presents the dramatic action of the story in two parts: an introduction, then a subsequent extended narration of the action under act headings. A writer includes the key elements of backstory in the introduction that are necessary for understanding the main characters, action, and theme. Included here would be the lingering, unsolved problem that will affect the immediate action. Only those characters and story elements that are critical for the story are described. For example, the introduction of the treatment for Witness would include Book, Rachel, Samuel, Captain Schaefer, and perhaps Eli; it would describe their appearance and nature, Schaefer's corruption, Rachel's loss of a husband, and Book's moral but violent character. Other characters and events are introduced briefly when relevant as the action is narrated under the following act headings.

Typically the introduction ends with a lead-in to the narrated action running something like this: "All seems well until this particular day, when someone sees or does or learns something that leads to the upheaval of his or her life." The introduction is usually two to three pages in length.

Then the dramatic action is narrated under act headings, scene by actual scene or sequence, as though the screenwriter has completed the screenplay and is now offering a detailed summary. The scenes are not numbered, dialogue is largely omitted, and camera language is entirely absent.

A screenwriter can indicate a character's feelings or thoughts and explain the importance of a given scene in a treatment, although all these elements must emerge directly from the action in the screenplay. A scene of some importance receives a fuller narration; a scene that is less important, but that contains important information, is narrated sparingly. No information is withheld from the reader, however ignorant the characters may be at the time in the action; the intent is to make everything clear to the reader—hopefully a producer who has purchased this story and expects the treatment to show how it really works.

At all times a writer emphasizes the developmental logic of the action and its relation to the theme, communicates the underlying act structure with its key turning points and revelations, and shows how the climactic action both resolves the conflict and drives home the essential point of the screenplay.

The action is narrated in the present tense: introduction and narration normally run about twenty-five double-spaced pages for a full-length screenplay. Length is not a virtue; clarity is.

Stepsheets and storyboards are also standard techniques sometimes used by writers to develop the action.

A stepsheet helps a writer chart each scene or sequence and their connection by asking Where? When? Who? What? Why? and How? for each. Where? sets the scene. When? establishes the time, always day or night. Who? lists required characters. What? indicates the action that takes place, including the complication or problem involved, the choice facing the protagonist, what decision is taken, and what changes occur. Why? lists the characters' motivation. How? indicates how this action motivates and leads to the next.

A storyboard is a series of sketches on a poster board with captions that show the progression of the key incidents of the action; it is typically used in preparing the production of a screenplay. Sometimes screenwriters adapt this technique into a more or less detailed variant of a stepsheet to sort out their own thinking. The sketches are kept simple.

3. Production Facts of Life

A play for the legitimate stage represents the uncompromised vision of a playwright. He cannot be replaced by another playwright, rewritten by committee, or dictated to by a director, producer, or star, as can a screenwriter. Consequently a successful playwright is still the most respected dramatist.

Theater enjoys two other superiorities to film. Plays receive multiple live performances; each live performance can bring out fresh nuances of character and conflict. A film is always the same, and even beloved films pall on repeated viewing. Plays also cost only a pittance to produce compared to films; a good play is likely to be produced many times.

The technical complexity of a film enormously complicates its production and expense, particularly with respect to elements of spectacle, and in consequence has long elevated the director and, until recently, the producer, over the screenwriter in credit. Yet a screenwriter makes much more than a playwright does. Few playwrights make a living from theater. Sometimes a screenwriter has a good relationship with a producer or director and therefore remains the one writer involved as a film is produced, maintaining his vision of the screenplay. Often, however, the original screenwriter is ignored after a screenplay is sold, others are brought in for revisions, and, if their revision is substantial enough, they will be given screen credit along with the original writer.

This use of multiple screenwriters is a major problem, for revision by committee leads to a bland and muddy product, since all good writing is expressive of a single governing vision. Sometimes collaborations do succeed, particularly in comedic writing, and many good films credit more than one writer—for example, *Witness, The Godfather* trilogy, and *Gone with the Wind* (for Sidney Howard had help with the script of that classic). *The Big Sleep* had three screenwriters, including William Faulkner, although it still takes many viewings to sort out the plot. Nonetheless, many films show this committee-generated blandness.

A corollary to this practice is a lack of respect for *writing*, with the consequence that Hollywood is famous for grand productions of clunkers, as well as the common garden-variety failures, which open and close without notice. Independent filmmakers suffer less from this problem, in part because their films often result from an intimate collaboration on a deeply felt story, as in *Taxi Driver*, the breakthrough film for Martin Scorsese, which was written by Paul Schrader. Ruth Prawer Jhabvala and James Ivory are a notable writer-director team of adaptations.

There are signs of change. Recently the screenwriter replaced the producer in the credits preceding the director. That will have to change, too: no film with a weak screenplay will ever be regarded as a great film, no matter how brilliant the production. The question that will always be asked in such a situation is, *What's it all for?* A great screenplay, competently produced, will always make an outstanding film. Since a lot of money rides on a film's success, in time even Hollywood will, in its crass way, accept the consequences of that fact.

Despite such problems, a screenwriter can safeguard his or her vision in a number of ways. First, by working with a director who respects his or her work; second, by ensuring contractually the right to make revisions, though it may be hard to make that exclusive. Even in ideal circumstances, however, a film is a collaboration, with the production team and the director making a far more crucial contribution than would be the case for the legitimate stage. For their contributions, the director and the production team of course deserve suitable credit.

Thus, the most certain way of maintaining a screenplay's integrity is for the screenwriter to direct the film. Many of the most outstanding screenwriters of the age have been directors, like Bergman, Bunuel, Antonioni, Kurosawa, and, on occasion, Truffaut. The screenplay author list at the end of this volume includes such current figures as Besson, Kieslowski, Coppola, and Towne.

Not all screenwriters will have the requisite talent to direct their work, nor will all want to do so. Such screenwriters must hope to work in a situation of respect and trust, but not be surprised when the opposite is the case.

4. Last Things: Manuals, Formats, and Perseverance

A deliberate effort has been made here to avoid all forms of jargon and to use only those terms that are traditional to the dramatic art, for nothing dates as swiftly as jargon. There may be special terms that crop up in the practice of specific genres—for example, in writing situation comedy for a given television show; such terms are few in number and can be left to specialized guides.

"Revisionist western" is a term in favor at the moment, referring to films like *Unforgiven*. It indicates only that a more realistic as opposed to an idealized treatment of theme and character is involved; the term will pass. "Sphagetti western" once referred to Sergio Leone films like *The Good, the Bad, and the Ugly;* now Leone's work is treated with more respect, and the term has become a curiosity.

Some jargon applies to plot language—like "plot points" for significant moments in the action, or "A" and "B" plots, used to differentiate the main plot from the subplot, usually among television writers. The problem is not with those who propound these terms but with the many who brandish them as a cloak for ignorance. Experienced screenwriters avoid jargon.

Some manuals have a "paint-by-number" quality, insisting that particular events must happen on particular pages. This is nonsense to be avoided.

That said, a world of manuals awaits anyone seeking a step-by-step guide to the dramatic art of screenwriting. An individual should feel free to use any that are found helpful: all of them are more or less aimed at beginners, and omit or simplify many of the elements reviewed here.

Most manuals review screenwriting format and camera language. Some computer programs automatically format a screenplay written to particular rules, but it is better for a beginner to avoid such tools and develop his or her own knowledge in these simple areas. Any computer word processor program will allow the creation of simple macros or styles that can take care of formatting and camera language.

Any screenwriter, whatever his or her talent or genius, needs to persevere. Screenwriting, like any writing art, is a lonely business. Producers, directors, actors, and production crews are able to practice their arts in communal proximity, but a screenwriter works alone. The activity of all these other contributors to the film becomes essential when the screenwriter's effort is finished, while at that point, except for revisions, he becomes superfluous. It is not a lifestyle to be entered idly.

Moreover, if a screenwriter ran an ad announcing the completion of a screenplay on a certain date, he would not find anyone at the door at the appointed time demanding to see his script. He must market his script directly or through an agent, with no guarantee of success. For every script that is filmed, thousands of scripts languish, while those filmed often are not the best, only the most faddish, or those that are filmed as the result of friendships or of mistaken estimation.

The old saying that Art is long, life short, remains true of all our major arts and artists. A good screenwriter writes from deep conviction, seeking the truth of our human condition and redeeming it by illusion as he educates, enlightens, entertains, represents, and provides a vicarious sense of mastery over the contents of our lives. Accomplishing this takes time to do well, and the result is always shadowed by the failure to reach perfection. Yet a good writer and his or her ultimate audience know that the laurels of genuine insight and accomplishment are beyond any price.

Notes

References to Aristotle are from the very readable S. H. Butcher translation, conveniently found in Francis Fergusson's *Poetics*. I am also familiar with the Ingram Bywater translation (in *The Basic Works of Aristotle*, ed. Richard McKeon [New York: Random House, 1941]), but do not cite it. Nietzsche's *Birth of Tragedy* is frequently referred to in the Golffing translation. Though translations of Nietzsche can be appallingly turgid, Golffing's work catches something of his fire and grace.

The following abbreviations are used in the notes:

AP: Aristotle. *Poetics*. Translated by S. H. Butcher, with an introduction by Francis Fergusson. New York: Hill and Wang, 1995.

BT: Nietzsche, Friedrich. *The Birth of Tragedy*. Translated by Francis Golffing. New York: Anchor Books-Doubleday, 1956.

PL: Plato. *Phaedrus*. In *The Collected Dialogues*, edited by Edith Hamilton and Huntington Cairns, pp. 475–525. Bollingen Series 71. New York: Pantheon, 1961.

1. Many artists have been anything but scions of health, although their creativity is doubtless their healthiest part. Creativity is subject to the same

perversions all other human activity is prone to, whether child pornography or the various, vicious propagandas of the twentieth century. To the extent that a creative response to experience is innate, as explored in I, 2 in reference to Kant, from one perspective, to function at all we must be creative. From another perspective, that creativity is amoral in the sense that it can be bent to any use. In what sense are creativity and health synonymous, then? The creative acts that strengthen and deepen our positive engagement with the world and our fellows are "healthy" in the way that we normally understand health within the particular culture and time that we inhabit. The creative acts that have a negative impact belong to the perversions. If this brings a certain cultural relativity to the second perspective from which we can understand creativity, so be it. In practical terms, we discriminate easily, for the most part, between when we use the world—or another person in it—badly or well.

2. I am indebted to John E. Pfeiffer, *The Creative Explosion* (New York: Harper and Row, 1982), for my comments on Paleolithic art.

3. When "Crisis" is capitalized, *the* crisis at the end of the Middle, or Act 2, is referred to; the "Climax" refers to the Act 3 climax. When "Beginning," "Middle," and "End" are similarly capitalized, the reference is to the overall beginning, middle, and end of a screenplay, or Act 1, Act 2, and Act 3.

4–11. Readers are referred to the works of Sigmund Freud, Carl Jung, Melanie Klein, and D. W. Winnicott, in addition to AP, BT, and PL. The texts listed below were particularly useful. References to the history of modern thought are drawn from a well-read but lay knowledge of philosophy. References to David Hume and Immanuel Kant are primarily to the works indicated below. For a brief, useful summary of Hume's work, see Dr. Justin Broackes's article in *The Oxford Companion to Philosophy,* edited by Ted Honderich (New York: Oxford University Press, 1995), pp. 377–81. For a similar summary of Kant's work, see Dr. Henry E. Allison's article in ibid., pp. 435–38. See also the following sources: Joseph Campbell, *The Hero with a Thousand Faces,* 2nd ed. (Princeton: Princeton University Press, Bollingen Series, 1968); David Hume, *A Treatise of Human Nature,* edited by L. A. Selby-Bigge (Oxford: Oxford University Press, 1888; reprint, 1960); Immanuel Kant, *A Critique of Pure Reason,* abridged and translated by Norman Kemp Smith (New York: Modern Library, 1958); *Prolegomena to Any Future Metaphysics,* translated and edited by Paul Carus (La Salle: Open Court Publishing, 1955); D. W. Winnicott, *Playing and Reality* (New York: Basic Books, 1971), p. 64.

There is a deep similarity between the hero pattern shown in Campbell's *The Hero with a Thousand Faces* and the pattern of dramatic structure as that is presented in the present text in the following chapters. If one straightens the diagram on page 245 of Campbell's text, the "Call to Adventure" and first threshold correspond to the Beginning, or Act 1, and its turning point; the hero's adventures/tests to the Middle, or Act 2, and the second threshold for "Return" to the Crisis; and the "Return" to the End, or Act 3. Although a given hero story or screenplay may well deal with only part of the overall hero myth, a screenplay always repeats the entire hero pattern *structurally,* leaving its hero and heroine enlightened and in some way fitter members of their community, which, on some level, they may have saved (as in *Star Wars*), or simply returned to with a deeper insight (*Witness*).

12. Both Robert Brustein's *The Revolt of the Theatre* and the works of Alois Nagler, the distinguished theater historian, are primary sources for I, 3. This material includes notes on Brustein's amplified lectures on the material covered in his work at the Yale School of Drama in 1966–67 and Nagler's endlessly useful and almost endless lecture notes on theater history and theory, also at the Yale School of Drama in 1964–67. Nagler's delivery was so perfected that he could predict to the minute in a lecture when a ponderous joke would arrive to provide comic relief.

13. Shakespeare's stage also contained a small inner stage that could change minimal sets behind a curtain, and an upper gallery, useful for battlement scenes or romantic scenes like the famous balcony scene in *Romeo and Juliet.*

14. References to Ibsen plays always refer to the Fjelde translations. The difference between Fjelde's versions and the bulk of the others available is similar to Golffing's superiority in Nietzsche translation. See Henrik Ibsen, *The Complete Major Prose Plays,* translated by Rolf Fjelde (New York: New American Library, Plume Books, 1978).

15. Ivor Montagu and Herbert Marshall, *Ivan the Terrible,* translated by S. M. Eisenstein (New York: Simon and Schuster, 1962), pp. 116–17.

16. Jean Cocteau, *Two Screenplays,* translated by Carol Martin-Sperry (Baltimore: Penguin, 1969), p. 9.

17. Television and videos may be watched in physical isolation or in limited intimacy with others. However, present in our consciousness at such times is the knowledge that we are part of a larger, anonymous audience of present viewers (television) or of past viewers (video). The atomization of the audience involved in these experiences is a separate issue.

18. This section is particularly indebted to Aristotle (AP, section 16), on

the types of recognition, or discovery. It is one of his more enduringly relevant contributions, though in need of updating.

19. This illusoriness is always the implication of our innate structuring of sensation, whether viewed through Kantian or evolutionary and biological lenses. However natural our sifting and structuring of sensation and impression may be physically and mentally, these innate structuring processes are characteristic of our particular functionality, and work well enough for practical purposes—but there is no guarantee that our mental structures are thereby an exact and unquestioned representation of the truth or that they are the same as those in other successful species.

20. Aristotle's discomfort with the irrational is apparent in the way he slides into technical issues (AP, section 25). The closest he comes to acknowledging the role of the irrational in creativity is his concession of the connection between metaphor and genius. He turns that discussion into technicalities too, essentially avoiding the issue that Plato deals with in PL and Nietzsche in BT. This inability to face the inherent irrational elements in creativity and drama impoverishes Aristotle and brings his catharsis theory dangerously close to superficial utilitarianism.

21. Aristotle insists only on unity of action (AP). The other unities are Renaissance inventions.

22. Nietzsche remarks on the breadth of mythological stories available to the Greek dramatists in BT, and the narrowness of their actual selection. Not all myths were tragic, of course, but even those were highly selected from, leading to frequent use of a narrow group of stories. His point is that human nature must be put under tremendous pressure to break it apart and see what makes it tick, and that such stories as Agamemnon or Oedipus are the ones that lend themselves to such an effort.

23. Shaw defended and popularized Ibsen to defend his own reform of dramatic practice. See George Bernard Shaw, *The Quintessence of Ibsenism* (New York: Hill and Wang, 1963), pp. 91–93.

24. Ingmar Bergman, *Fanny and Alexander* (New York: Pantheon, 1982), p. 155.

Screenplay Author List

The following lists the screenwriters of those films mentioned in the text; a **D** indicates that the author also directed the film. A bare * denotes that the work was not filmed.

An Affair to Remember, 1957
Delmer Daves, Leo McCarey **D**

Agamemnon
Aeschylus *

Alfie, 1966
Based on the play by Bill Naughton
Bill Naughton

Alien, 1979
Dan O'Bannon

The American President, 1995
Alan Sorkin

The Bacchae
Euripides *

The Battleship Potemkin, 1925
S. M. Eisenstein **D**

Beauty and the Beast, 1946
Jean Cocteau **D**

Beauty and the Beast, 1991
Alan Menken, Howard Ashman

Beetlejuice, 1988
Michael McDowell, Warren Skaaren

Beowulf
Anonymous Anglo-Saxon epic *

Beyond Rangoon, 1995
Alex Lasker, Bill Rubinstein

The Big Easy, 1987
Dan Petrie, Jr.

The Big Sleep, 1946
William Faulkner, Jules Furthman,
Leigh Brackett

Bird, 1988
Joel Olianksy

The Birdcage, 1995
Based on *La Cage Aux Folles*
Elaine May

The Blood of a Poet, 1930
Jean Cocteau **D**

Blue, 1993
Krzysztof Kieslowski **D**, Kieslowski
Piesiewicz

Born Yesterday, 1950
Based on the play by Garson Kanin
Albert Mannheim

Born Yesterday, 1993
Based on the preceding film
Douglas McGrath

Breathless, 1959
Jean-Luc Godard **D**

Brubaker, 1980
W. D. Richter, Arthur Ross

Casablanca, 1942
Julius J. Epstein, Phillip C. Epstein,
Howard Koch

Chinatown, 1974
Robert Towne

Citizen Kane, 1941
Orson Welles **D**, Herman J.
Mankiewicz

Clash of the Titans, 1981
Beverly Cross

Cleopatra, 1963
Joseph L. Mankiewicz **D**

Cool Hand Luke, 1967
Frank Pierson

Cries and Whispers, 1972
Ingmar Bergman **D**

Cross Creek, 1983
Based on the memoir by
Marjorie Kinnan Rawlins
Dalene Young

Cyrano de Bergerac, 1996
Based on the play by Edmund
Rostand
Jean-Paul Rappenau **D**, Jean Claude
Carriere

Dances with Wolves, 1990
Based on the novel by Michael Blake
Michael Blake

Dave, 1993
Gary Ross

A Doll's House
Henrik Ibsen *

Donnie Brasco, 1997
Based on the book by Joseph O.
Pistone with Richard Wooley
Paul Attanasio

Dr. Zhivago, 1965
Based on the novel by
Boris Pasternak
Robert Bolt

The Eiger Solution, 1975
Based on the novel by Trevanian
Warren B. Murphy, Hal Dresner,
Rod Whitaker

The Emerald Forest, 1985
Rospo Pallenberg

Emma, 1996
Based on the novel by Jane Austen
Douglas McGrath **D**

The Eumenides
Aeschylus *

Falstaff
Giovanni Verdi *

Fanny and Alexander, 1983
Ingmar Bergman **D**

For Your Eyes Only, 1981
Michael J. Wilson

The Four Feathers, 1939
R. C. Sherrif, Lajos Biro, Arthur
Wimperis

Four Weddings and a Funeral, 1994
Richard Curtis

Frankie and Johnny, 1991
Based on the play by
Terrance McNally
Terrance McNally

Gandhi, 1982
John Briley

Ghosts
Henrik Ibsen *

Glory, 1989
Kevin Jarre

The Godfather I, II, III; 1972, 1974,
1990
Based on the novel by Mario Puzo
Mario Puzo, Francis Ford
Coppola **D**

Godzilla, 1955
Takeo Murate, Inoshiro Honda

Goldeneye, 1996
Jeffrey Caine, Bruce Feirstein

The Gold Rush, 1925
Charles Chaplin **D**

Gone with the Wind, 1939
Based on the novel by
Margaret Mitchell
Sidney Howard

*The Good, the Bad, and
the Ugly,* 1967
Sergio Leone **D**

The Graduate, 1967
Buck Henry, Calder Willingham

Hair, 1979
Based on the Broadway musical by
MacDermot, Ragni, and Rado
Michael Weller

Hamlet
William Shakespeare*

Henry V, 1944
Based on the play by
William Shakespeare
Laurence Olivier **D**, Alan Dent

Henry V, 1989
Based on the play by
William Shakespeare
Kenneth Branagh **D**

High Noon, 1952
Carl Foreman

High Plains Drifter, 1972
Ernest Tidyman

Independence Day, 1996
Roland Emmerich, Dean Devlin

Ivan the Terrible I, 1944
S. M. Eisenstein **D**

James and the Giant Peach, 1996
Based on the novel by Roald Dahl
James Kirkpatrick, Jonathan
Roberts, Steve Bloom

Jeremiah Johnson, 1972
Edward Anhalt, John Milius

Johnny and Frankie, 1992
Terrance McNally

Jurassic Park, 1993
Based on the novel by
Michael Crichton
David Koepp, Michael Crichton

Jurassic Park: The Lost World, 1997
Based on the novel by
Michael Crichton
David Koepp

Kagemusha, 1980
Akira Kurosawa **D**

King Lear
William Shakespeare*

King Solomon's Mines, 1950
Based on the novel by
H. Rider Haggard
Helen Deutsch

Kramer vs. Kramer, 1979
Based on the novel by
Avery Corman
Robert Benton **D**

La Cage Aux Folles, 1978
Frances Veber

La Femme Nikita, 1991
Luc Besson **D**

Last of the Dogmen, 1995
Tab Murphy **D**

The Last of the Mohicans, 1992
Based on the James Fenimore
Cooper novel and the 1936
version of the film
Christopher Crowe, Michael
Mann **D**

The Last Temptation of Christ, 1988
Paul Schrader

Lawrence of Arabia, 1962
Robert Bolt, Michael Wilson

Lethal Weapon 1, 1987
Shane Black, Jeffrey Boam

Lethal Weapon 2, 3, 1989, 1992
Jeffrey Boam

Little Caesar, 1930
Based on the novel by W. R. Burnett
Francis Faragoh, Robert E. Lee

A Man for All Seasons, 1966
Based on the play by Robert Bolt
Robert Bolt, Constance Willis

Measure for Measure
William Shakespeare *

Medicine Man, 1992
Jerry Goldsmith

The Merry Wives of Windsor
William Shakespeare *

A Midsummer Night's Dream, 1968
William Shakespeare
The Royal Shakespeare Company's
performance, filmed

Mrs. Doubtfire, 1993
Randi Mayem Singer, Leslie Dixon

Much Ado About Nothing
William Shakespeare *

Much Ado About Nothing, 1993
Based on the play by
William Shakespeare
Kenneth Branagh **D**

My Fair Lady, 1964
Based on *Pygmalion* by George
Bernard Shaw
Alan Jay Lerner

Never Cry Wolf, 1981
Curtis Hanson, Sam Hamn

Nixon, 1995
Christopher Wilkenson, Stephen J. Rivele, Oliver Stone **D**

Norma Rae, 1979
Harriet Frank, Jr., Irving Ravetch

Oedipus Rex
Sophocles *

On the Waterfront, 1954
Budd Schulberg

Oresteia
Aeschylus *

Orlando, 1992
Based on the novel by
Virginia Woolf
Sally Potter **D**

Othello
William Shakespeare *

Othello, 1952
Based on the play by
William Shakespeare
Orson Welles **D**

Othello, 1995
Based on the play by
William Shakespeare
Oliver Parker **D**

The Outlaw Josey Wales, 1976
Philip Kaufman

Out of Africa, 1985
Kurt Luedke

Pale Rider, 1985
Michael Butler, Dennis Shryack

The Piano, 1993
Jane Campion **D**

The Prince of Tides, 1991
Based on the novel by Pat Conroy
Pat Conroy, Becky Johnston

Prizzi's Honor, 1985
Based on the novel by
Richard Condon
Richard Condon, Janet Roach

The Professional, 1994
Luc Besson **D**

Pygmalion
George Bernard Shaw *

Radioland Murders, 1994
Willard Huyck, Gloria Katz,
Jeff Reno, Ron Osborn

Raiders of the Lost Ark, 1981
George Lucas, Philip Kaufman

Ran, 1985
Based on *King Lear* by
William Shakespeare
Akira Kurosawa **D**

Rashomon, 1951
Akira Kurosawa **D**

Rear Window, 1954
John Michael Hayes

Remains of the Day, 1993
Based on the novel of
Kazuo Ishiguro
Ruth Prawer Jhabvala

Return of the Jedi, 1983
George Lucas, Lawrence Kasdan

Richard III
William Shakespeare *

Richard III, 1995
Ian McKellen, Richard Longcraine

A River Runs Through It, 1992
Based on the novella by
Norman MacLean
Richard Friedenberg

Rocky, 1976
Sylvester Stallone

Romeo and Juliet
William Shakespeare *

Romeo and Juliet, 1962
Based on the play by
William Shakespeare
Franco Zeffirelli **D**

Roots, 1977
TV Miniseries
Based on the book by Alex Haley

Roxanne, 1987
Based on *Cyrano de Bergerac* by
Edmund Rostand
Steve Martin

Samson and Delilah, 1949
Jesse L. Lasky, Frederic M. Frank

Scarface, 1983
Oliver Stone

Schindler's List, 1993
Based on the novel by
Thomas Keneally
Steven Zaillian

Sea of Love, 1989
Richard Price

Seven, 1995
Andrew Kevin Walker

Shane, 1953
Based on the novel by Jack Schaefer
A. B. Guthrie, Jr.

Shogun, 1980
TV Miniseries
Based on the novel by James Clavell

The Silence of the Lambs, 1990
Based on the novel by
Thomas Harris
Ted Tally

Sleepless in Seattle, 1993
Jeffrey Arch, Larry Atlas, David S.
Ward, Nora Ephron **D**

Smiles of a Summer Night, 1955
Ingmar Bergman **D**

Spartacus, 1960
Dalton Trumbo

Speed, 1994
Graham Yost

Stargate, 1994
Dean Devlin, Roland Emmerich **D**

Star Trek: The Search for Spock, 1984
Harve Bennett

Star Trek: The Wrath of Khan, 1982
Jack B. Sowards

Star Wars, 1977
George Lucas **D**

A Streetcar Named Desire
Tennessee Williams *

A Streetcar Named Desire, 1951
Based on the play by
Tennessee Williams
Tennessee Williams

Suddenly Last Summer, 1959
Based on the play by
Tennessee Williams
Gore Vidal

Suspect, 1987
Eric Roth

Taxi Driver, 1976
Paul Schrader

The Tempest
William Shakespeare *

Tender Mercies, 1983
Horton Foote

Tightrope, 1984
Richard Tuggle **D**

Time After Time, 1980
Nicholas Meyer **D**

To Kill a Mockingbird, 1962
Based on the novel by Harper Lee
Horton Foote

Tootsie, 1982
Larry Gelbart, Murray Schisgal, Don
McGuire

Two Mules for Sister Sara, 1970
Albert Maltz

2001: A Space Odyssey, 1968
Based on *The Sentinel* by
Arthur C. Clarke
Arthur C. Clarke, Stanley Kubrick **D**

Unforgiven, 1992
David Peoples

The Usual Suspects, 1995
Christopher McQuarrie

Victor/Victoria, 1982
Based on the 1933 German film by
Reinhold Schunzel
Blake Edwards **D**

The Virgin Spring, 1959
Ingmar Bergman **D**

War of the Worlds, 1953
Based on the novel by H. G. Wells
Barre Lyndon

Waterland, 1992
Based on the novel by Graham Swift
Peter Prince

Witness, 1985
Earl W. Wallace, William Kelley

The Year of Living Dangerously, 1982
Based on the novel by C. J. Koch
Peter Weir **D**, David Williamson

Z, 1969
Constantin Costa-Gavras **D**